Ice Princess

Based on the screenplay by Hadley Davis
Novelization adapted by Suzanne Weyn

SCHOLASTIC INC.

New York Toronto London Auckland Sydney
Mexico City New Delhi Hong Kong Buenos Aires

ISBN: 0-439-74552-7

Adapted from "ICE PRINCESS," a Walt Disney Pictures feature film
release. Screenplay by Hadley Davis. Story by Meg Cabot and Hadley Davis.
Executive producer William W. Wilson III. Produced by Bridget Johnson.
Directed by Tim Fywell. Copyright © 2005 Disney Enterprises, Inc.
Used by permission. All rights reserved.

12 11 10 9 8 7 6 5   5 6 7 8 9 10/0

Designed by Jennifer Rinaldi
Printed in the U.S.A.
First printing, April 2005

WALT DISNEY PICTURES PRESENTS

Ice Princess

Chapter 1

"Casey! Can I see you?"

Science lab was over and I was nearly out the door when my physics teacher called me. *Uh-oh!* I thought. I did a quick mental check, searching for something I might have done wrong, but I came up blank. "Is there a problem, Mr. Bast?" I asked, stepping back into the lab.

He raised his hand, signaling me to wait, as he removed one slice from a wrapped package of sliced bread on his desk. He took it to a lab table and lit a Bunsen burner. Then he grabbed the slice with lab tongs and began toasting it before answering me.

"Nothing's wrong," he said with a smile. "I was just curious if you've begun weighing your college options."

"My *options*," I said, repeating his word. Options were choices and I wasn't sure what mine were yet. "They're going to be, ah, pretty much dictated by the price tag," I explained. By that I meant I would be attending the college or university that awarded me the biggest scholarship.

He nodded and turned his bread over. "Have you ever heard of the Helen Stoller Physics Scholarship?"

"No," I replied. Ever since I became a junior in high school last September, I'd started researching science scholarships. Science was my best subject and I figured if anything was going to win me college money that would be it. But I'd never heard of a Helen Stoller Scholarship.

"It's given to a student from this part of the state who shows the most promise in physics," Mr. Bast explained, still toasting.

My mind raced. My best friend, Ann, was great in physics and so were a few other kids in my class. I was up there with them, but was I the *best*?

Mr. Bast seemed to read my thoughts. "I'm talking about you," he said. "You have a calling, Casey."

"I do?" I questioned, not even quite sure what a *calling* was. "What is it?"

"Physics!" he cried excitedly, waving his tongs. "Toast?" he offered.

"Uh, sure," I replied. We were talking through my lunch period and my stomach was growling. Even toast sounded good right then.

Mr. Bast went back to his desk and opened a drawer. Inside was a jar of strawberry jam. "You're very lucky," he continued as he opened the jar. "Most people search their whole lives to discover their calling."

I realized that by *calling* he meant the thing that I was destined to do with my life, my reason for being on the planet. "But how do you *know* if something's your calling?" I asked.

"When your brilliant teacher tells you so," he replied, handing me the toast with jam. "And, of course, your eleven straight A pluses on exams is a hint."

"Wow . . . I have a calling," I said, pleased. It sounded kind of cool.

"Indeed, you do," Mr. Bast confirmed. "To compete for the scholarship—which you can use to attend whatever college or university you choose—you will need a letter from me and you should think about a special physics project over the summer."

"What kind of physics project?" I asked.

"It should be something unusual but personal," he said. "Let them know you a little. The student with the project that is considered the best will win the scholarship."

I thanked him and hurried out of class, munching on my Bunsen burner toast. This was really exciting. If I won this scholarship I could add it to the scholarship money I hoped to get from a college and maybe my entire tuition would be paid.

It would solve a huge problem. My mom really values education and she's been stressing over how she was going to be able to pay for my college ever since I started high school.

Lunch was nearly over by the time I reached the cafeteria. My friend Ann was leaving just as I arrived. She saw me and waved, hurrying over to meet me. "Why did you miss lunch?" she asked.

I told her what Mr. Bast had said about the Helen Stoller Scholarship as we walked out into the hall together. "He said physics was my calling and that he'd write me a letter of recommendation," I added. "But you're as good at physics as I am."

Ann shook her head. "Not even close," she disagreed. "I grind while you glide." I understood what she meant. Ann has to study much harder to get her good grades than I do. Physics just makes sense to me. I suppose I have a logical mind.

Ann suddenly stopped short and gripped my wrist. Following the direction of her gaze, I spotted Kyle Dayton, a hockey-playing senior-class hottie, coming toward us. We just stood and stared at him, probably looking like two fools, as he walked right past us without even noticing.

Ann kept her eyes on him until he turned the hallway corner. "One day that guy is going to wake up and realize he needs a math tutor," she said dreamily, "and that tutor will be me."

With Kyle Dayton out of sight, Ann's mind unclouded and we were able to talk about the scholarship again. I didn't know how I would ever be able to get this special, brilliant, and personal project done in time to compete for it.

My schedule for the summer was already jammed up. I had a long reading list for the Advanced Placement English class I was taking in my senior year, and my mom had already paid for me to attend an S.A.T. class to raise my college application test scores. I'd taken the test already and done well, but Mom wanted me to aim for Harvard University. That meant taking the test again and scoring even higher.

We continued talking as we turned the hall corner. "And even if I chase this scholarship," I told Ann, "I have no idea what the topic of this project could be!"

Ann didn't comment and, looking up, I realized she was distracted by the sight in front of us. A small crowd of what you might call the "popular kids" was gathered together. Blond, gorgeous Gen Harwood was handing out small envelopes, probably invitations, to the cheerleaders, football players, and other "cool" kids in her clique of friends.

In the next minute something truly bizarre and unexpected happened. Gen looked in my direction and smiled.

Not that there's anything wrong with me, but I'm your average-looking, thin, mousy type. The most "cool" thing about me is the two blond streaks in my light brown hair, which no one believes are natural, even though they are. What was strange about Gen smiling and coming toward me was that she never before, ever, had given any indication that she realized I existed.

And then I noticed something even stranger still. Gen seemed to be slowly extending an invitation out to me. This couldn't be happening. Yet, it was!

"Hey, you're Casey, right?" she asked, still smiling. I nodded, totally stunned as she handed me the invitation. "This is an invite for my boyfriend's party," she said.

"Wow," I murmured. Maybe I had somehow been transported into a parallel universe where this sort of thing actually happened. It was far-fetched, I knew, but it was the only possible explanation.

"You're in chem lab with Aaron Hennings, aren't you?" she continued. "Can you give that to him? Thanks!"

Unfortunately, *that* was another explanation—a much more likely one. She just wanted me to deliver the invitation for her. I should have known better.

Gen breezed off down the hallway, leaving me holding the *so not mine* invitation. "That was way inconsiderate," Ann commented.

I agreed.

That evening, I told Mom about the Helen Stoller Scholarship as we set the table for supper. "I love Mr. Bast!" she shouted enthusiastically. "If he uncovered a scholarship I didn't know about, he's a genius!"

Mom then started to ramble on about how they don't pay teachers enough and that their contributions aren't sufficiently valued by society. She was getting so worked up that she was slamming the plates down on the table.

I knew that if I wanted to discuss the scholarship with her I'd have to somehow get her back on the subject. That's how my mom is. She gets sidetracked and forgets what we're talking about. "Mom," I prodded.

"I'm back. Sorry," she apologized, putting her hand to her chest and breathing deeply. At least she knows how she is and tries to control it.

"Look, I don't know what he's talking about," I told her, getting out two glasses from a kitchen cabinet. "What's a *personal science project*? Isn't the nature of science supposed to be, like, completely unbiased and factual? I mean, now they want *spin,* too?"

"Harvard wants everything," Mom said.

I lifted the pot on the stove and smelled something delicious. "What's in here? Meat?" I asked. Most of the time meat is too expensive to fit into Mom's budget.

"Yeah, well, Dad's check actually came this month," she explained. My parents are divorced. It happened so long ago that I don't really remember him. He lives far away and he doesn't visit. My dad is supposed to send Mom a child-support check every month. Some months it comes and a lot of months it doesn't.

Over dinner we talked more about the scholarship. "I'll help you find a project," Mom offered.

"Mr. Bast says it has to be *personal,*" I reminded her. "I have to do it myself."

The scholarship project was still on my mind as I sat down to watch the National Figure Skating Championships on TV that night. Ann had come over to watch them with me. We both love figure skating and wouldn't have missed this event for anything.

Before long, though, I'd forgotten all about my

scholarship worries as I became swept up in the excitement of the competition. One of our favorite skaters had just launched a spectacular triple jump.

The familiar voice of the skating commentator came on, analyzing every moment of her leap into the air. "She reaches back . . . she overrotates . . ."

I stood up anxiously, suddenly realizing that she might not land the jump. "Ohh!" I shouted in disappointment as Sasha fell and slid along the ice on her butt.

"She just couldn't hang on to that landing," the commentator said sadly.

"She had it locked up!" I cried, flopping back onto the couch. We watched with admiration as she got right back up and continued her routine as if the fall hadn't happened. "Look at this recovery," I pointed out. "Amazing! She'll still place."

They showed her jump again in such slow motion that it resembled a wire frame computer image. "She's so precise," I murmured, concentrating on the slo-mo playback.

An idea was beginning to form inside my head. "You know what?" I said to Ann, my eyes still riveted on the TV set. "I bet there's an exact aerodynamic formula for that jump."

"What?" Ann asked, not getting my meaning.

It didn't matter. I knew what I meant. There had to be a way, using formulas in physics, to analyze a skater's jump and predict if it would land correctly or not. I mean, I wasn't positive it could be done — but it seemed to make sense.

"Yes!" I cheered quietly. I felt pretty sure I had come up with a project!

Chapter 2

Once I came up with the idea, I couldn't wait to get started on my project. The closest skating arena was the Harwood Rink, so I rode my bike there early the next Saturday morning.

My heart thumped nervously as I entered and walked down the linoleum floor of a hallway lined with photos of skaters. I adjusted the strap of my day-pack that held Mom's video camera, one of the few luxuries she'd ever bought for us.

I entered a doorway at the top level of bleachers and gazed down at the dimly lit rink at the bottom. No one seemed to be there even though the front door hadn't been locked.

Then—*BAM!*—bright fluorescent lights clicked on and the ice suddenly shone like a diamond. It was as if, in an instant, the rink had come to life.

Music kicked in next as three female figure skaters dressed in pretty practice outfits skated out. I drew in a quick breath of awed amazement.

To me, this was like a whole other world—a world that only existed on TV. In my life, skating meant bundling up and going out to a nearby pond. It was something I loved to do, but the ice was bumpy and the wind blew me around. It was nothing like this bright, smooth-as-glass indoor rink.

I continued down the bleacher stairway until I was behind the boards. I was as close to the ice as I could be without actually standing on it. The three skaters moved like graceful, magical ice princesses—so confident and lovely as they spun and leaped through the air, practicing their routines.

My fantasy bubble burst in the next minute, though, when I realized that these *princesses* were girls I went to school with.

I didn't know them personally, but I knew their names. One was an elegant, well-dressed Asian-American girl named Tiffany Kwong. The petite redhead was Nikki Sellman. And the gorgeous blond was none other than nasty Gen Harwood.

I suddenly put it together. Gen Harwood . . . the Harwood Rink . . . someone in Gen's family probably owned the rink! How cool was that?! She had her own rink!

Remembering why I had come, I took the video camera from its case and began to film the practice. Almost immediately, Nikki did an amazing move called a triple toe loop. It was just the type of thing I'd come here to film and I'd captured every bit of it. I was still filming when the camera was suddenly jerked away from me.

A blond woman in her thirties stood in front of me, red-faced with fury, gripping my camera in one hand. "*WHAT* do you think you're doing!" she demanded angrily. "Why are you filming my skaters?"

She was so enraged that I didn't know what to say. "It's, ah . . . my . . . my physics project," I stammered out my explanation.

The woman ignored this. "You're scoping her triple loop. Why?!"

"I . . . uh . . . want to analyze the movement," I tried to tell her.

She was an attractive woman, for an adult in her thirties, but the disdainful, disbelieving smirk on her face just made her look mean to me. "Who are you working for?" she asked me accusingly.

"Nobody!" I cried. Why wouldn't she believe me?!

"Teddy!" she called to a young guy in the bleachers who was repairing one of the seats. "Come down here!"

He was very large and was holding a huge wrench

in his hands as he headed toward me. "Keep her here," the woman instructed him. "I'll call the cops."

Call the cops! "No!" I shouted. "I'm a student! Look! Here!" I rummaged desperately in my pack and pulled out a notebook. "Look at this," I pleaded.

The woman just glared at me so I handed it to the guy, who, I realized, was not much older than me. I hoped that since he was young he might be more understanding. "I didn't think there would be a problem," I said as I pressed the notebook into his hands. "I thought this was a public rink."

"Private practice only from six in the morning until ten," the woman said in a nasty growl. "These girls are training for the Regional Championships—which I think you know perfectly well!"

I went back into my pack and pulled out my student ID. "I'm a student, really," I said.

The guy began paging through my notebook. It was filled with physics problems and graphs. "Whoa! Definitely spy code," he told the woman. At first I didn't get it. What was he talking about? Then I realized he was joking.

Gen Harwood had spotted us and skated over. "What are *you* doing here?" she asked disdainfully. I guess when she no longer needed me to do her a favor she couldn't bother to be nice.

"You know her?" the woman asked Gen.

Gen nodded. "She's a science geek."

The woman looked me up and down. For the first time, I got the feeling she was starting to believe my story. I tried to smile confidently at her but all I could muster was a nervous little grin. "I just want to digitize some images into my computer and see if any kind of unified theory emerges," I explained in a small voice.

The woman wrinkled her forehead and frowned, as if I were speaking a different language and she didn't understand a word of it. I suppose what I'd just said *did* sound pretty science geeky.

Then, all at once, her expression relaxed. "Okay, look," she said. "If Gen knows you and you want to take some notes, I don't care. But you'll have a hard time convincing the parents."

I wondered what parents had to do with this.

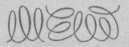

By the end of the session, two parents, Tiffany's dad and Nikki's mom, had come in and were staring at me suspiciously. Out on the ice, the coaches kept looking my way curiously. By filming the practice I'd learned that the woman who had been so angry at me was Gen Harwood's coach. The other two girls had coaches of their own.

At the end of the session, the woman, whose name

I learned was Tina, suggested that I explain to the parents and coaches why I was there. Putting away my camera, I took a deep breath and attempted to tell them what I wanted to do for my project. "I'll enter the data into a Maya program and—" I began.

"What program?" Nikki's mom, a large, heavily made-up woman interrupted.

"A high-level software for creating and editing three-dimensional graphics and animation. Like movies with special effects in them use," I told them. "With this I can study things like the inference angle of the blade entering a jump and its effects on velocity and height—"

"No," Nikki's mom broke in again. "The only authorized film footage of Nikki appears on her Web site, www.TeamNikki.com. I charge people ten-ninety-five a month to watch her lutz. We got ten thousand hits last month."

"And ninety-eight-hundred of them were you," Tiffany's dad cracked. Nikki's mom just glowered at him. I'd had no idea that these parents were going to be so intense and competitive.

"None of this footage will ever be seen outside the scholarship committee," I assured them.

"No talking to my daughter," Tiffany's dad warned. "She's training. No distractions."

"Not a word. No," I promised.

A surge of happiness ran through me. No one seemed to have any other objections. This sounded like they were agreeing to let me film.

Gen had skated up and came off the ice. "Look, I don't care if you're here," she said. "But if you post me on the school Web site falling on my butt, you'd better transfer to another school."

The next morning I was at the rink super early with my video camera, filming all the skating action. I filmed Tiffany doing an amazing spiral sequence. Gen spun so fast she became a blur of movement and Nikki's jumps were mad awesome.

At one point I became so involved in what I was doing that I stepped out onto the ice to get a better shot. Immediately, a voice shouted at me. "Hey! No street shoes on the ice!"

It was that big guy, Teddy, the one with the wrench from the day before. I definitely did not want to mess with him so I got off the ice quickly.

Luckily I had brought my beat-up old skates, just in case I needed them. I quickly laced them up and got back out on the ice with my camera.

Actually, it turned out for the best because I found that I could really get the film footage I needed when

I was closer. I skated around the girls and in between them, filming from every angle.

I noticed Gen's coach, Tina, watching me closely as I skated. I kept expecting her to shoo me off the ice, but she didn't. The way she kept staring made me a little uncomfortable about my skating. Mostly, though, I was too into filming to really worry about her.

One time, while I was filming Gen in the middle of a spin, she suddenly became distracted and lost her balance, sprawling onto the ice. I was sure I'd be blamed, but instead Tina shouted up at a guy standing in the bleachers. "Brian! She's training! You know the rule!"

Looking up at him, I recognized Gen's boyfriend. He held up something in a wrapper. "I just brought her something to eat," he said.

Gen got up and skated to Tina. "But, Mom, can't I take a half-hour break?"

"Not if you want to win," Tina refused.

It took a second to sink in, but I realized that Gen had called her Mom. Up until that moment I hadn't known that Gen's coach was also her mother.

"Hey, Mrs. Harwood," Brian called. "You should coach our basketball team. We could use a kick in the butt."

"If you don't leave this instant, that's exactly what you'll get!" Tina shouted back at him.

Brian left and Gen started practicing again. If my

project had been on studying body language I would have gotten some good footage. She did all her moves perfectly but she held herself tight with anger, clearly furious.

Tina didn't seem to care how angry her daughter might be. "I do not want him coming here during practice, do you hear me?" she said firmly.

"But I never get to see him!" Gen argued. "Other girls—"

"You're not like them, Gennifer," Tina insisted. "Winners make sacrifices!"

"Or maybe they just cheat," Gen shot back.

That last remark really stung Tina; I could see it as I filmed her shocked expression. Then, suddenly, she whirled around and looked directly into the camera. "Turn that off!" she shouted at me.

Chapter 3

$\mathcal{B}$y the end of the week, I'd fed images into the program and studied them closely. Using all my knowledge of physics, I'd done my best to apply formulas to the skaters' movements. Even though I'd really worked hard on writing up my project—I'd included graphs, the formulas, and the digital images—I was nervous when I finally gave it to Ann to read.

We met in our favorite coffee shop and I ate while she read. I worried about what she thought of my conclusion. "The conclusion is too simplistic, isn't it?" I asked anxiously before she even finished the last page. "The kinetic energy in a jump equals half the skater's mass times velocity squared minus—"

"No!" Ann cut me off. "I don't know if it's simplistic or not. I could barely understand it!"

I looked at her, puzzled. From her admiring tone of voice it seemed as though she meant this as a compliment. Was she implying that if she couldn't understand it, it must be brilliant?

That couldn't actually be a good thing, could it? I mean, Ann was very smart. If she couldn't understand the project maybe it was just . . . unclear.

Then an uneasy look came into Ann's eyes. I know her well enough that I realized she was about to say something she really didn't want to have to say. "I don't know if they'll care," she began cautiously, "but it's . . . just a little bit . . . dry."

She didn't want to say it and I didn't want to hear it—but I knew she was right. What I'd written *was* very technical and probably pretty dull, too. "A little dry," I repeated her words. It was exactly what the scholarship committee *didn't* want. "Mr. Bast said to make it personal. How do I do that?"

Ann shrugged. "I don't know. Put more *you* in it."

More *me,* I considered as I chewed my pencil. How could I get more of me into this project?

I was already on the ice, right there with the skaters. If there was any more *me* in the project I'd actually have to do the moves myself.

My eyes suddenly widened as the idea hit me. That was it! I'd do the moves myself!

But could I do it? Was that even possible?

Then another idea came to me. There just might be a way I could make this work!

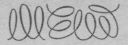

I caught up with Tina Harwood in the rink parking lot when I knew practice was over and she'd be heading to her car. "Excuse me, Tina . . ." I said, hurrying up to her.

She turned and looked at me with a questioning expression. Tina wasn't someone I found easy to talk to so I just plunged right in, blurting out what I'd come to say. "Is there any way I could take a few lessons? I think I might be able to write a little better about some of these principles if I'm the one actually applying them, so if there's any way—"

"Fine," she interrupted me. "We're starting a novice-level class for the summer session. That's three afternoons a week, eight hundred dollars."

"Eight hundred dollars!" I gasped. She might as well have said eight million!

There was no way that was happening!

Maybe, though, we could work something out. "Well, I don't need a whole session," I pressed on. "It would be really cool if I could, like, work on my form for a single loop and maybe a lutz."

Tina seemed amused by what I was suggesting. "It doesn't work like that," she said, shaking her head. "You can't just order one from Column A and one from Column B." She continued walking to her car and I followed. "You're not a bad skater. Let me know if you change your mind."

She drove away and left me there thinking about what she'd said. That conversation had not gone at all as I'd hoped. And, in one way, it had been a total bust. But she'd said I wasn't a bad skater. Was that why she'd been staring at me while I filmed?

It was just the little bit of encouragement I needed right then. Plan A had failed so it was time to come up with Plan B.

My Plan B was to ask Mom for the eight hundred dollars. It was an almost instant failure. So I immediately went to Plan C—getting a job to pay for the lessons myself.

Summer vacation had begun and I was free to work during the day. I spotted an ad in the paper that said the Harwood Rink needed a responsible person to work behind the counter of their snack bar.

How perfect was that!?

It would have been *completely* perfect if it wasn't for the hairnet. The net they required me to wear over my hair was hideous, a total humiliation, and the snack bar manager totally insisted that I wear it because of some health code. So I put it on and tried not to think about how horrendous I looked.

It was a small stand with only three stools in front of it. Skaters could buy hot and cold snacks that they ate from paper plates using plastic forks. It was always jammed with hungry, impatient people and it seemed I was never able to serve them fast enough.

One day Gen Harwood came up to the stand. She, naturally, looked all cool and gorgeous with her blondness back in a French braid, wearing her cute practice outfit. And I . . . well . . . I was wearing a hairnet and lunch-stand uniform.

"What are you doing here?" she asked as Nikki and Tiffany came up behind her—each also looking great in her own way.

"Um . . . working," I replied, "for my science project."

"Aren't you going a little overboard with this project?" Gen asked.

To be honest, she was only asking the same question I'd asked myself several hundred times already. Somehow, though, I couldn't admit it to her. This whole situation was humiliating enough as it was. Instead, I tried to sound completely confident. "Well . . ." I began. "I'm completely committed to it, just like you guys are committed to your skating."

"Whatever," Nikki said, dismissing me with a wave

of her hand. "I'm starving. BLT here, hold the B, heavy on the L."

Tiffany gave me her order, speaking so softly that I had to strain to hear her. "Beef patty, no bun," she requested.

"Salad for me," Gen added. "Just put in iceberg lettuce, half a cup of garbanzo beans, and a lemon wedge. Since it's Saturday, I'll splurge and say add a quarter cup of cheese to the salad."

"Ooohh, cheese," Nikki teased Gen.

"Coming up," I told them. I realized that all of them were watching their weight even though you couldn't find three girls more slim and fit-looking.

I put their orders together while they talked at the counter. They acted like I wasn't even there, but I couldn't help overhearing their conversation.

"I don't know what's wrong. I'm popping my lutz," Gen told them, looking worried.

"It's all that cheese you've been eating," Nikki joked.

"My father noticed I gained," Tiffany said sadly, not joking one bit.

"He noticed a quarter pound?" Nikki asked in disbelief.

Tiffany nodded. "He says I'm not serious enough. I've got to focus more. I heard Zoey Bloch's been sticking a quad." I knew she was talking about a quadruple jump, a very spectacular move.

"That's a rumor," Gen scoffed, "and she probably started it herself."

"It's kind of early in the season for stupid head games," Nikki complained.

"Not for Zoey," Gen said. "She stole Chantal DeGroat's skates at the Regionals."

"Re-ally," Nikki said, drawing out the word to underscore her keen interest in this. "I heard it was her mother who did it."

I delivered their salads and they took them without a word of thanks. The only one who even spoke to me was Gen, who complained that I'd given her too much cheese as she picked most of it out of the bowl.

I thought about the things I'd overheard them talking about. I could see how deadly serious, even sometimes ruthless, these three skaters were. I wondered if all skaters were this way.

After they left, I hurried to get my kitchen clean-up work done. As soon as my shift at the snack bar was over, I'd start my first figure skating class. Even though I hadn't earned the full eight hundred dollars yet, my employer had agreed to take it out of my earnings. She could do that because, as it turned out, my employer, the owner of the rink, was also my new skating teacher—Tina Harwood.

Chapter 4

$\mathcal{I}$ don't think I could have felt any more geeky and out of place than I did that day as I skated out on the ice in my jeans, bulky sweater, and beat-up old skates. The class consisted of ten little girls and one little boy, probably between the ages of four to seven. And then there was the matter of my outfit—or lack of outfit, I should say. All of them were dressed in sleek workout clothes and gleaming new skates.

Finally, there was the fact that, even though I was the oldest one, I was clearly the least experienced. They all moved confidently across the ice, some of them practicing simple ballet moves on the ice even though this was supposed to be a beginner class.

"Are you a substitute teacher?" a little girl of about six demanded to know in a disapproving tone, her hands on her slim hips, "because my mom paid for Tina and if Tina's not teaching us, then—"

"I'm a student!" I said quickly, not wanting to hear any more from the tiny tyrant. "Really—just like you guys."

"You're kidding!" said the one little boy, who looked to be five years old. "What are you—thirty!?"

"Sixteen," I replied.

The little boy smirked and waved his hand at me dismissively. "You're over!"

"I didn't start skating until I was five," the demanding little girl put in, "and *that* was late."

"Too late to compete," the boy agreed.

"I'm not in this to compete," I told them. I had to bite down on my laughter at the shocked, appalled looks that came to their small faces when they heard *that*.

Tina appeared on the ice, not wearing skates, and walked toward us. "All right, everybody," she announced. "Welcome to our Snowplow Sam class. Let's line up."

As we got in a line, Gen skated over to us breathlessly. "Class, can you tell our teacher's assistant the most important rule of this class?" Tina asked, glowering at her daughter.

"Use the bathroom before class?" a little girl offered.

The rest of the class already knew the correct answer and sang it out in unison. "Never be late!"

Gen started to apologize to her mother. "Sorry, I was—"

Tina turned away from Gen and addressed the class. "We've got a lot to do if we're going to be ready for our recital in August. We're going to work on our toe loop . . ."

Gen demonstrated a toe loop.

". . . our lutz . . ." Tina continued as Gen did a lutz for the class.

My jaw dropped slightly. Gen was really an awesome skater.

"But first," Tina went on, "you all have to get comfortable throwing your bodies in the air." She then turned to me. "Casey, you're the physics whiz—what's the rule about what goes up?"

That was an easy one. "Newton's Law of Gravity," I answered. "What goes up must come down."

"Right!" she agreed. "So grab some Styrofoam." She and Gen began handing out thick Styrofoam pads attached to Velcro belts. They were just right for little kid-sized butts, and although I wouldn't call my butt overly large, it was definitely not kid-sized anymore. Gen skated by and handed me two pads. I hoped that would work.

Even though I'm a decent skater, jumping was completely new to me. Other than doing the occasional cartwheel, I didn't usually leap up into the air and hope to land on my feet, and certainly not on one thin blade. So, I guess it wasn't too surprising that I spent a lot of the session sprawled on the ice. The other kids in the class fell, too, but not as often or as gracelessly as I did.

Finally, after about a zillion attempts, I threw myself high into the air and actually wobbled down on two feet next to the bossy little girl I'd spoken to earlier. "Could you try to, like, not *squish* me?" she scolded.

"Sorry," I apologized breathlessly.

"Casey, you've got to pull your arms in," Tina advised as she walked toward me. "They're throwing you off balance."

I nodded and tried the jump again, this time pulling my arms in tightly to my side. Once again I came down on my blades and this time it was a much smoother landing.

"Now try that about five thousand more times," Tina said as she walked off to assist another student.

"Right," I muttered. I watched the other kids attacking their jumps with total concentration and intensity. They were so little and yet they were completely focused.

The little boy did a jump I thought was amazing. I opened my mouth to tell him what a good job he'd done when another voice boomed out from the side of the rink. "Jeremy," a woman yelled, "that toe pick is there for a reason! You dig it in or no TV for a week!"

The little boy, Jeremy, bit his lip and tried again. I couldn't believe his mother had been so harsh with him.

The bossy little girl skated past me, gliding on one leg with the other extended behind. "This is a lot of pressure for a recital," I commented to her.

"It's only everything," she replied coolly. "The whole point is that you've got to pass the USFSA-JST."

"The who's-what?" I asked.

"The U.S. Figure Skating Association's Juvenile Skating Test," she informed me. "It's the first step in qualifying for the Regionals. I mean, for us kids—*you* don't have to do it."

"That's good," I muttered as we went back to practicing our jumps, "because it's not possible."

The three hours of class seemed like an eternity. By the time it was over, I'd fallen on my butt about a thousand times. The two pads I'd strapped on were shredded and falling apart. A trail of little Styrofoam crumbles leaked out everywhere I went. But by the end of class I was able to land a still-slightly-shaky single loop and—I have to say—I was pretty pleased with myself.

I was the last one to skate off the ice and was just at the boards when a huge machine rumbled into the rink. The word ZAMBONI was written across the front of it.

I stared, transfixed by the magical way the Zamboni machine created ribbons of fresh, clean, gleaming ice everywhere it went. I'd heard of machines like these but never actually seen one.

As the Zamboni rumbled past me, I got a look at the driver. It was Teddy, the guy I'd met on the first day. His expression was sort of dreamy, as though driving this huge machine was his idea of happiness. He looked like a completely different guy. For the very first time, it occurred to me that he was kind of cute.

He drove the machine in a wide oval and, little by little, the entire rink began to shine with clean, smooth ice. The glistening surface was so inviting that I just couldn't resist testing it out. I turned back and stepped out onto the rink, gliding along. It was incredible!

"ARE YOU OUT OF YOUR MIND!!"

The shout startled me and I slammed into the side boards, completely out of control. Bouncing off the boards, I went down and spun on my side.

Teddy had climbed off the Zamboni and was running over to me. "Don't you know anything?" he shouted. "No skating when the Zamboni is out! That thing could squash you!"

He leaned down to help me up, but he was back to

being the scary, crabby guy I was used to. And I was back to being scared of him. "No thanks," I said, waving him away. "No, no . . . I'm fine."

I struggled to my feet, but as soon as I got up, my knees buckled. I lunged toward the boards and grabbed on for support.

"Ohh . . . you're fine. Ohhkay," Teddy scoffed as he walked away.

He was probably right that I'd been stupid to go out onto the ice while he was working. "I'm sorry," I called out.

He turned back to me and his expression was slightly softer. "You want to tell me what was in your head?" he asked, clearly mystified as to what could have compelled me to do something so dumb.

"I've never skated on such a smooth surface before. I wanted to see what it was like," I revealed.

"Lake skater?" he asked.

"Pond," I told him as I attempted to skate off the rink. Once again, I wobbled badly and had to grab the boards in order to stay up.

Teddy extended his hand to me. "Okay, look, you need some help."

"No! No!" I refused, waving him off. "I'm good to go." My next attempt to skate away ended abruptly as my knee buckled and my leg slid out from under me. I landed hard on my butt. The Styrofoam pads couldn't take it anymore and exploded in a shower of Styrofoam bits.

Up until then I'd thought that being the big gawky beginner in the skating class of sleek little figure skaters was the most embarrassing thing that had ever happened to me. I'd been wrong. *This* had to be the most mortifying, humiliating moment of my life.

As long as I was already down, I decided to stay down and began picking up the Styrofoam bits. "You really must want that A," Teddy remarked as he got on his knees to help me pick the small nubs off the ice.

"It's not for an A, it's for a physics scholarship," I told him while we worked together.

"What, like inertia, and drag, and velocity, and all that?" he asked.

I looked up at him, surprised. "How did you know about that?"

"I'm into cars," he explained. He jerked his head toward the Zamboni. "I get this baby out on the road, I can open her up to . . . oh, seven miles an hour. She'll blow the doors off any street sweeper in town."

Once again he was the happy guy I'd seen driving the Zamboni before, not scary at all. We continued to work until all the tiny pieces were up. "I should get home," I said when we were done.

"Yeah, you should," he agreed.

I looked at him quizzically. What had he meant by that? I thought we'd sort of become . . . friendly.

"I can't do the ice until you're off," he explained, reading the question in my eyes correctly.

"Right," I said, laughing at myself. "Sure. Well . . ." The little rest I'd taken while picking up Styrofoam enabled me to skate away without falling.

I watched him walk back to the Zamboni and I was surprised to find that I felt sort of sad to see him go.

Chapter 5

hat night my muscles ached horribly. Yet my mind was racing and I was too excited about my project to sleep.

Trying to do the jumps myself had been exactly the right thing to do. It had given me a much more personal understanding of what muscles were used and how much pre-takeoff speed was required. In just one day I'd gained a whole new appreciation of what was required to become a competitive skater. It was insanely hard work!

Based on this new understanding, I decided to reexamine my skating images and analyze them again. I was still working on creating new formulas when Mom looked in on me at about one in the morning.

"How's it coming?" she asked.

"It's coming," I replied, looking back and forth from my computer screen to my notebook as I jotted down equations.

She stood behind me and looked at the image on the screen. It showed Gen doing a triple toe loop. "I know it takes incredible training and effort and there's all this artistry involved," she said, "but, I'm sorry, I just can't get past those twinkie little outfits."

I checked the picture. Gen was wearing a leotard with a very short ruffled skirt at the hips. "Mom, that outfit is actually aerodynamically sound," I told her.

Wearing heavy or flowing clothing creates what physicists call *drag*. In its simplest terms, drag refers to air resistance—the less drag, the faster something, including a skater, can move through the air. It's easier for a skater to move smoothly if he or she is wearing sleek, streamlined clothing.

Mom is a very smart woman, but English literature is her field of expertise, not physics. She sees things in terms of themes and plot development rather than aerodynamics; therefore she didn't care a bit about the lack of airborne drag in a skater's outfit.

"Those outfits set women back fifty years," she insisted. "If I saw you squeezed into one of those things, I'd probably cry."

"Mom, you never will," I assured her.

She smiled at that and kissed the top of my head. "Go to sleep sometime, okay?"

"Okay," I agreed, reasonably sure that I'd go to sleep eventually.

For the next three weeks I worked at the snack bar from morning until late afternoon, and then I hit the ice. Three days a week I went for my lesson and on the other four days I practiced. Being Tina Harwood's student entitled me to unlimited practice time on the rink and I took advantage of every second of it.

I was learning fast, too, because Tina was a great teacher. She was able to pinpoint just the thing her students were doing wrong and knew exactly how to correct it.

Sometimes it felt like I was progressing only inches forward at a time, but at the end of each week I realized I was a much better skater than I'd been the week before.

Before I knew it, it was nearly time for the recital.

Since I wasn't planning to compete, I decided I wouldn't participate. I figured I'd spare myself the embarrassment of being the biggest skater and the worst one there.

One day, in the rink, as Tina handed out costumes, I told her that I wasn't going to be in the recital. "Oh, so you're nervous," she said.

"I'm not!" I protested.

"No, I get it," she insisted knowingly. "It *is* harrowing, getting up there in front of all those people."

"Tina, I'm in a baby class," I reminded her. "I don't think there's anything to get scared about."

Tina shot me a skeptical look. "Everyone gets scared—every time," she said.

It annoyed me that she just assumed she knew how I felt—better than I knew myself! Even though I respected Tina as a teacher, I still didn't like her. She was probably the toughest, hardest person I'd ever met.

One afternoon, I asked Ann to come to the rink so she could film me as I skated. I hoped that if I included a film of myself skating and explaining my project, it would help make the whole thing seem more *personal*.

Since shoes weren't allowed on the ice, Ann had to skate out with the video camera and she was pretty wobbly. While she struggled to stay steady, I struggled to seem perky and confident on camera.

"Hi! I'm Casey Carlyle!" I chirped into the camera, like some out-of-control talk show host. "And I've decided to see if I could prove my own hypotheses on the application of physics to the required elements of competitive figure skating. First let me demonstrate a single flip that does *not* work."

Ann continued filming as I skated quickly enough to pick up the speed I needed to attempt a single flip. Instead of trying to do it correctly, I intentionally kept my upper body loose, my legs tight, and leaned too far forward. As I expected, the flip didn't get very high and I only managed a shaky landing.

"That pretty much blew," Ann commented.

I skated back up to her and spoke into the camera. "Now I'm going to increase the centripetal force by tucking in my arms. This will decrease my moment of inertia, enabling me to spin faster. I'll increase the height of my jump by applying more force to my toe pick."

Skating back out into the rink, I picked up the speed I needed. I planted my toe pick properly this time and leaped high. I pulled my upper body in tight and landed a more-than-decent flip.

"Okay!" Ann cheered. "Now let's see you push it!"

"What?" I asked.

"Let's make it dramatic! We need the thrill of victory, the agony of defeat!" she shouted excitedly. "This video is boring. Make it exciting!"

"Okay," I said, accepting her challenge. "Watch this!"

I skated fast, faster than I'd ever skated before. As long as the camera was on, I decided to give it all I had. At the very least, she could film the "agony of defeat." Leaping into the air, I realized I was going really high. I spun—and spun again! The extra height I'd reached allowed me the time for the extra spin.

I didn't want to think about falling out of my landing,

not from this height. And—to my complete shock—I didn't. I stuck it.

I'd done a perfect double flip!

I guess Ann was as amazed as I was. She lowered the camera and just stared at me with her mouth open.

My heart was hammering in my chest. It was partly from the effort of doing the double flip, but it was from excitement, too. I'd just accomplished something amazing and all of a sudden I wanted to show everyone what I could do!

Chapter 6

The next day I couldn't wait to get to the rink and talk to Tina. I arrived as soon as the rink opened and found her in her office. "I'll do it," I said. "The recital. I want to do it!"

I'd thought about it the whole night before. Landing a perfect double flip had filled me with confidence. Tina's assessment had been right, after all. I had been afraid to skate out there in front of an audience, but I wasn't frightened anymore.

Tina pushed her chair away from her desk and stared at me for a moment. "Well, this is about as last minute as it gets," she remarked. "You know that you have to be here tonight by five-thirty?"

I hadn't realized I'd need to arrive so early. "I've got a Harvard Tea at three," I said. It was something Mom had signed me up to do—an event where I would meet teachers and students from the Harvard science department and they would get to meet me.

"Then what are we talking about?" Tina asked impatiently.

I thought fast, calculating the time it would take to get home, change, and arrive at the rink. If *nothing* went wrong, I could make it . . . just barely. "I'll get there," I assured her.

Tina beckoned me to follow her down the hall to the locker room. She opened a large metal trunk and began rummaging through the skating costumes inside. "I think most of these would cut off your circulation," she decided, lifting out a too-small sequined leotard before tossing it back in.

Hands on her hips, she studied me a moment. "Come to my house at noon today," she said. "One of my old things might work on you."

"What old things?" I asked, not understanding what she meant.

"Just be there," Tina said, walking away.

I looked up Gen's address in our online school directory and biked to the Harwoods' house at noon. Gen wasn't home but Tina was waiting for me. She'd pulled out several competitive-skating outfits and laid them out on the couch. She picked one that looked like a good fit. "Wear this and don't be late," she said, handing it to me and steering me toward the front door as though trying to get rid of me quickly.

As soon as I got home, I ran upstairs to my bedroom and tried on the outfit. Wow! I barely recognized myself. I was certainly the last person who ever expected to see me dressed in a bright red figure skating costume with mesh and cutouts and a zigzagged flame on one side. But there I was—in my bedroom trying on exactly that outfit.

I didn't know whether to be pleased or horrified with this new me in the mirror. It was so . . . not me. And yet—I had to admit it—I looked pretty good.

There was a knock on my door. "Sweetie?" Mom called.

I jumped guiltily. When I'd told Mom that she'd never see me in a "twinkie" skating outfit, I'd meant it sincerely. But I hadn't known then that I'd soon be able to land a perfect double flip. "Just a sec!" I replied, pulling a robe on over the outfit and tying it tightly. "Okay!"

She came in holding a large shopping bag. "I have a surprise!" she announced excitedly. She pulled a flowered skirt out of the bag and tossed it on my bed. A fitted jacket followed the skirt onto the bed. "I bought it for you to wear to the tea today," she said. "I can't wait to see you in it."

The red skating outfit may have been not me,
but—in a totally different way—the skirt and jacket
Mom bought me were even *less* me. I looked like some
kind of junior corporate executive. I hated it, but I
couldn't tell that to Mom and hurt her feelings.

She was still raving about the skirt and jacket as
we climbed the steps to a mansion on the Harvard
campus. "I think the whole effect is very grown-up,
but there's a passing nod to femininity," she gushed.
"You're going to be mingling with lots of other future
classmates and professors. I really wanted the look to
say, 'We are serious!'"

"It definitely succeeds," I said glumly.

As Mom opened the front door to the mansion she
suddenly stopped and hugged me. "I'm just so happy
that you're going to this tea," she explained as she let
go. "I was so worried! I mean, you've been *living* at
that rink. I thought you were getting all distracted and
it was cutting into your focus on Harvard."

We went inside where the large room was already
filled with many students and professors, all mingling
and chatting pleasantly. A tall girl wearing a name tag
that read PENELOPE came over to say hi. Mom told her

that I was interested in physics and her eyes lit with enthusiasm.

"Physics rocks!" she cried. "In sophomore year you can join the Quantum Club. And that rocks because we get to compete against Cal Tech, M.I.T., and Stanford! Last year our ion particle accelerator took first place! It rocked!"

"Sounds really . . . rockin'," I commented, not knowing what else to say. This girl seemed nice but, I wondered, did I really want to be around people who just lived for physics?

"If you have time right now, I can take you through the entire physical sciences syllabus," she offered.

Oh, joy, I thought.

Mom clapped her hands in delight. "That would be wonderful. We have nothing but time!" she cried as I anxiously checked my watch.

By the time I rushed breathlessly into the rink it was after six. Tina glowered at me angrily, but luckily she had too much else to do so she couldn't focus on me.

By seven, the bleachers were packed with spectators, mainly the family and friends of the Snowplow

Sam class. A panel of three United States Figure Skating Association judges sat at a table along the side of the rink, waiting to observe.

I stood behind the boards with the rest of the class and Tina, ready to skate out. The moment the lights dimmed and the music came on, nervous sweat immediately sprang to my forehead. Tina must have noticed it. "I told you," she reminded me. "It happens every time."

"What do you *do*?" I asked, feeling helpless against this attack of nerves.

"Deep breaths," she advised.

The little kids skated out first and looked completely adorable in their costumes. They were amazing as they performed their routines, although Jeremy fell one time.

As I watched them skate, I concentrated on my breathing, trying to keep it deep, slow, and calm as I prepared to go on. Finally, it was my turn to skate out onto the ice.

I built speed as I went through the required elements that the kids had just done—single jumps, an axel, a lutz, a single toe loop. I managed to hang on to all of them without falling, except that I did a clunky two-footed landing on my toe loop. I hoped I could make up for it with a flip.

Summoning all my determination, I skated fast and jumped. Yes! I landed the single flip cleanly. The crowd applauded.

And then I did something that surprised even me. I followed the single flip with a double flip!

The audience cheered and I couldn't stop smiling! Off to the side, Tina looked impressed. Even Gen, beside her, nodded in grudging approval.

I spotted Teddy sitting on the parked Zamboni. He was clapping and cheering along with the rest of the audience.

The little kids all skated out to the center of the rink while the crowd continued to applaud. I joined them in taking our bows as a class.

The judges sat at their table scribbling feverishly. They were assigning the pass or fails to the students.

We skated off and went into the locker room. As we unlaced our skates, Tina came in with the results. They were written on cards and she handed them out without comment.

The bossy little girl from my class, whose name was Lilly, cheered as she read her result. "Novice—pass! Yes!" She turned to me, smiling. "Casey, how'd you do?"

"Fine, I guess," I told her, reading my card. "It says junior pass." I figured the word PASS was a good sign but I didn't understand why it said JUNIOR and not NOVICE.

I was still studying my card when I realized it had suddenly gotten quiet. What was happening?

Everyone in the locker room was staring at me. The kids, Tina, Gen—all of them were looking at me with shocked expressions.

"What?" I asked.

"You skipped two levels!" Lilly blurted.

Whoa! I blinked hard at her. Was she kidding?

"That's where Gen and Nikki and Tiffany are," she went on.

When Lilly said that, Gen shot me a frosty glare that made me think it might actually be true. But it was too unbelievable. "Tina, is it true that I'm on a junior level now?" I asked.

"Yes, it's true," she confirmed.

"So if I . . . wanted to compete . . ."

Tina didn't even let me finish the thought. "You can't," she said.

I didn't understand. "Why not?"

Tina took my arm and walked me away from the crowd. "All that happened tonight was that the judges saw the same thing I've seen all summer—you've got some raw talent," she told me in a low, serious tone of voice. "But that's not enough to have a shot at the Regionals. You need a coach, ballet teacher, choreographer, and private ice time. Nikki's parents took out a second mortgage just to put her through this. Tiffany's father works two jobs."

I hadn't realized any of this, not at all.

Tina pointed down at my skates, which I was still wearing. "They're falling off your feet," she pointed out. "You need custom Harlicks—six hundred dollars *minimum*—and you need to have the blades sharpened every six weeks and—"

She saw from the bummed look on my face that I totally got it.

"I'm sorry," she said. "It just is what it is. Believe me, competitive figure skating isn't something you do on a whim."

"How do you do it for Gen?" I asked.

"Well, she saves on a coach and choreographer," she pointed out.

I supposed it really helped to have a mother who could do those things. Suddenly, it hit me. Tina had all those costumes from her past. She herself skated like a champion. "You were good, weren't you?" I said.

Tina shrugged, as if she didn't want to talk about it.

"How far did you get?" I asked.

Tina looked away, definitely not wanting to discuss her past as a competing skater. "Come back to the rink and visit us when you get the chance," she said.

The locker was suddenly flooded with parents, hugging their kids. Tina went off to talk to them.

She left me standing there with my junior pass, which would get me exactly nothing. How had this wonderful evening suddenly turned into such a complete bust?

Chapter 7

The last weeks of summer flew by as I scrambled to do all the things I'd neglected because of skating. I read the required books on my summer reading list and took the S.A.T. prep course. Before I knew it, it was September, time for my senior year of high school to begin.

I'd also kept my job at the Harwood Rink snack bar. It was pretty painful being there without being able to skate, but I tried not to think about it. Since Tiffany, Nikki, and Gen skated before I came in I didn't see them. That helped keep my mind off competitive figure skating, at least.

On the very first day back at school, I spotted Gen, Nikki, and Tiffany standing together off to the side of the front entrance. I figured they'd just ignore me so I was pretty surprised when Tiffany spoke. "I heard you landed a double," she said and then began to applaud.

Gen nudged her, as if to say, "Why are you talking to *her*?"

But Tiffany kept on. "It took me two years to do that," she revealed.

"Really?" I asked.

The three of them began to move toward the front door. "So, I guess we'll see you," Nikki said.

"Well, no, you won't," I replied, "not at the rink. I can't train with you guys."

"Why not?" Tiffany asked.

"I can't get together the goodie package," I admitted, trying not to sound as bummed by this reality as I felt. "So . . . it was fun," I added with a resigned little wave of my hand.

I expected them to walk off but, to my surprise, they fell into step with me as I entered the school. Even more surprising was what Gen said next. "Look, I'll tell you something, okay? You don't know how lucky you are."

That was a shocker! "Why am I lucky?" I asked as the four of us continued walking into school and down the busy hallways.

"You're lucky to have a life," she said.

"You think I have a life?" I asked.

"I know you do," she insisted. "You have TV time, friend time—"

"But you get to skate all you want," I reminded her.

"*More* than I want," she corrected me. "I'd love to be you. You're free to do what you want on Saturday night—"

"You get to eat sugar," Tiffany added.

"Oh, boo hoo! Who cares about going out or about eating sugar," Nikki said. "Don't you just want to skate all the time?"

"No!" Tiffany and Gen answered at the same time, their voices overlapping.

Nikki studied them, shaking her head disdainfully. "What's the matter with you two? Are you insane?"

I could see that she meant it. Obviously she loved the skating life. But I was totally unprepared for what Gen and Tiffany were saying. I'd assumed they loved it, too. Apparently I'd been mistaken.

"If I bobble even one landing, nobody speaks to me all through dinner," Tiffany complained.

"Then stop bobbling," Nikki chided her. "Get a grip!" She turned on her heels and headed off to her class alone.

"She's a good competitor," Tiffany said, watching her walk away.

"The best," Gen agreed.

We'd come to my first-period classroom. "Well, bye," I told Gen and Tiffany. "This is my physics class."

"Physics? Wow!" Gen said. "I can't even pass math."

"You never know until you try," I said as I entered the class.

Mr. Bast was my teacher once again. He smiled when he saw me, which I took as a good sign. I'd mailed him the written part of my project a week earlier and I hoped his pleased expression meant that he thought it was good.

After class, he asked me to stay. He smiled again as he took my report from his top drawer. "This is exactly what the scholarship committee is looking for," he said.

"I'm finishing up the CD-ROM that goes with the report so they can see the results with a real skater," I told him. "Well, not a real skater," I corrected myself. "It's me."

"I bet there are some pro skaters out there who wouldn't mind taking a look at this, either," Mr. Bast remarked.

"You're kidding," I said. Did he really think it was *that* good?

"No, I'm not kidding," he assured me. "It seems like the kind of thing that could really help them up their game. And, just think—it's not even illegal."

He stood up and offered his hand to shake. I was glad he thought so highly of my project, but that wasn't the only reason I was smiling. He'd just given me a very exciting idea.

I didn't waste any time turning my idea into action. That same day I asked both Tiffany and Nikki to ask their parents and coaches to meet me late that afternoon at the Harwood Rink. Of course, I knew Tina would already be there.

The reason I made the appointment late was that I needed time after school to go home and do some calculations on my computer. The first thing I did was study a photo image of Nikki doing a sit spin. She traveled on that spin—which wasn't good—but I was pretty sure that I had a physics formula that would help her stop doing that.

Next, I analyzed some film I had of Gen wobbling as she landed a double axel. I was pretty certain I could figure out a formula that would explain why it was happening and would also reveal the best way to correct it.

Working feverishly, I scribbled down a whole bunch of formulas as I studied more footage. Finally, by four-thirty, I grabbed my laptop and hurried out of my bedroom. Strapping it to my bike with two bungee cords, I rode to the Harwood Rink as fast I could pedal.

I found Tina in her office and asked if I could make a short presentation to her and the other parents. "Sure," she agreed, looking completely mystified.

When the other parents arrived—Tiffany's mother and father and Nikki's mom—I began. I explained to them about the report I'd written and told them how Mr. Bast had suggested that my calculations might help real skaters.

Turning on my computer, I showed them how the Maya program had helped me analyze their daughters' moves. "Once you understand the aerodynamics and moment of inertia, the timing and arm positions can be better calculated," I explained. "This would give you an edge—excuse the pun—that none of the other skaters have."

Looking up from my laptop, I didn't see the enthusiastic, appreciative expressions I'd expected.

"Look, we don't have time for this voodoo," Tiffany's dad said dismissively.

Tiffany's mom pointed to the computer and sneered. "This is just a cartoon!"

Only Tina seemed to appreciate what I was trying to do. Her eyes bored into me searchingly. "What do you want?" she asked.

Chapter 8

"She's back!"

I had just landed a single toe loop in the middle of the rink and looked up into the bleachers to see Teddy there. "How'd you get the rink time?" he asked.

"Physics!" I told him happily as I skated the rink, preparing for a single flip. Tina was also in the bleachers watching me. I wanted to impress her and decided to double the flip.

Tina had agreed to give me rink time if I'd analyze Gen's skating moves. Her interest had swayed the other parents as well. I'd offered to trade for things with them, too, but they'd said they would have to think about it.

When my rink time was done, I went into the locker room. I was starting to unlace my skates when Nikki came rushing in. I'd asked if I could use some of Nikki's choreography in exchange for analyzing her skating. Now I couldn't wait to hear what her mother had decided.

"She said absolutely not," Nikki told me. "She goes, 'The Jumping Shrimp does NOT share her choreography with the competition!'"

"The Jumping Shrimp?" I asked.

"It's my trademark. Mom copyrighted it," Nikki revealed. "We're marketing plush shrimp dolls and everything."

Nikki was fairly tiny and her jumps were excellent, so I supposed the name fit. Personally, though, I would not like being referred to as a *shrimp*.

"Anyway," Nikki went on, "I convinced her that I could teach you my last year's program. I mean, it's old, but who cares, right?"

Actually, I cared—a lot. Did I really want to learn some old routine everyone had already seen? But maybe we could set it to different music and change the order of the moves. It sounded like the best deal I was going to be able to make. "Right," I agreed. "Who cares?"

There was one giant unknown in all this—I didn't know for absolute certain that it would work.

In theory, my formulas were supposed to tell exactly how a particular move should be performed in order to assure a perfect outcome. The formula was an ideal, intended to be compared against how the skater was *actually* performing a certain move. The idea was that the skater could then improve her performance by making certain corrections. In *theory* the skater's performance would improve because she would now be moving in a way that was more aerodynamically efficient.

But was I right about my theory?

Were my formulas correct?

I was about to put them to the test, and if I was wrong, my rink time and choreography would quickly disappear.

Fortunately, though, it looked like I had done my work correctly. After Nikki looked at my computer image of a perfect flying sit spin and I explained to her what she was doing differently, she improved one hundred percent.

The spread-eagle sequence in Tiffany's routine improved almost overnight after I used physics to see what she was doing wrong. Tiffany couldn't stop thanking me.

Gen was harder to convince when I went out with her on the ice to work on her double axel. She was having a lot of trouble landing it and nothing would

Thanks to a recommendation from my physics teacher, I have the chance to get a scholarship for college! I filmed the skaters at the ice rink as research on the physics of skating.

But the more I filmed, the more I wanted to skate myself. To pay for lessons, I took a job at the ice rink snack bar.

In class I was clearly the least experienced—even though the other students were under seven years old!

I overheard Gen, Tiffany, and Nikki talking at the snack bar and wondered if all skaters were as serious as they were.

At the recital I did something that surprised even me. The judges were so impressed that I got a junior pass!

Gen advised me on how to cope in the Regionals and helped prepare me for the competition.

"Do you want to blow this scholarship to become a professional athlete?" Mom asked me angrily. "Something's got to give! Do you want that something to be Harvard?"

The pond surface was bumpy until Teddy smoothed it out with his Zamboni.

The competition was tough—Nikki and her mother were serious about winning.

I put in many hours of practice: ballet lessons, workouts, and exhausting training sessions with Tina at the rink.

Why didn't Mom understand that it was always going to be the Casey-and-Mom show?

Glancing into the bleachers, I saw that I had a small fan section. Teddy and Gen were there to watch me skate.

Tina had told me to "skate with my heart" and so that's exactly what I did.

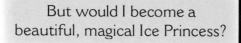
But would I become a beautiful, magical Ice Princess?

make her believe that a scientific formula would make any difference. But Tina insisted, so she gave it a try.

I gave her some pointers that were based on principles of physics and my analysis of the way she was performing the move. After listening and viewing the computer image, she raced around the rink and then took off!

Up in the air she went for one, then two revolutions. By doing it my way she gained the height she'd been lacking and she came down gracefully.

"It worked!" I shouted happily, feeling more than a little amazed and very relieved.

"You told me it would," she reminded me. For the first time ever, she actually smiled at me. It was a great smile, too, full of pure happiness.

Chapter 9

On the next Saturday afternoon as I was cleaning up the snack bar kitchen, Gen came in and asked if I wanted to hang out with her. I suppose I shouldn't have been completely shocked by the request. Nikki, Tiffany, and Gen had all been pretty friendly to me since the first day of school. And now that I was helping them train, we were almost . . . *friends,* sort of.

Still . . . me hang out with Gen Harwood? Our social worlds didn't exactly overlap. In fact, I didn't even have a social world that I could think of. Even though I was exhausted, how could I say no?

So that's how I came to be at a backyard party full of kids I barely even knew. They were all from Gen's crowd—cheerleaders, members of the various teams. Gen actually dragged me over to meet Kyle Dalton, the super hottie that Ann was hoping to someday tutor in math!

"Casey, Kyle," she introduced us. "Kyle plays hockey, and Casey, you skate. So you two have a lot in common. Have fun!"

Seeming satisfied that she'd left me well connected, she rushed away. I saw her melt into the arms of Brian, her boyfriend.

I was starting to get the picture. I was the cover to get her out of the house so she could be with Brian.

I might have felt used and insulted, except that there I was, sitting next to Kyle Dalton. How bad could I really feel? "So, you skate, huh?" he asked.

"Figure . . . skate," I answered, trying to get my nerves under control. He really was cute!

"I wouldn't let the team hear this, but you guys could skate circles around us," he said. Wow! He was nice, too.

"But I'm not pushing a puck," I pointed out, feeling more comfortable.

"You should come to our next game," he said. Had Kyle Dalton really just invited me to come watch him play hockey? It seemed that—unbelievable as it was—he had.

I was about to tell him that I'd love to come watch him play—but I was suddenly distracted by a guy who was whooshing above us on a zip-line that had been suspended across the backyard. "WOOOOOO!!!" he cheered as he zoomed past.

"Uh-oh, he's not going to make it," I realized.

"Sure he will," Kyle disagreed.

I shook my head, studying the guy, who continued to shout happily as he clutched the triangular blue handle he rode on. "No," I insisted. "Assuming his weight to be 150 pounds, and at that rate of descent, his projected trajectory brings him—"

Kyle and I cringed as we heard a terrible crash right behind us. Turning, we saw that the guy had smashed right into the patio furniture, overturning two chairs and landing in a painful-looking position underneath the table.

"It brings him right there," I said to Kyle. "It was a simple V times M equals A miscalculation."

From his bewildered expression, it was pretty obvious that he had no idea what I was talking about. "You know," I added, trying to explain, "velocity times mass equals acceleration. Physics."

He began slowly backing away from me, clearly seeking a way to escape the crazed brainiac he now realized I was. "I have to . . . um . . ." he stammered. "Uh . . . later," he said before hurrying away.

A group of "cool" girls had witnessed the entire event and stood staring at me like I was the biggest loser of all time. "That was Kyle Dayton," one of them informed me with chilly disdain, as if I didn't know the caliber of the prize I had just driven away with my smart-girl babble.

"Word of advice," said another of them. "Don't ever talk again."

"Sorry," I said, feeling like as big a geek as they thought I was. "I can't help it. When I get nervous I babble a little. Actually, I babble a lot. It's like a gear comes loose in my brain and just like one of those Planck diagrams of random particles colliding out of control—"

"Um . . . you're doing that babbling thing again," one of the girls pointed out, her lip curling into a scornful sneer.

"I think babbling is hot."

We all turned at once to see who had spoken. Teddy walked up to me and took my arm, walking me away from the crowd of jeering girls. "Thanks," I said, sighing with relief. I jerked my head toward the girls. "Do they eat small rodents for breakfast?"

"I think they just chew glass," he said, laughing.

We walked together into the house, where kids talked and danced. "See, I don't go to many parties," I explained. "Well, no parties, really, at all, unless you count birthday parties—but who counts birthday parties? I mean, they're mandatory and they're usually mine. You can't count your own party, can you?"

"Hey, Casey, it's me," Teddy said gently. "You can stop now."

I took a deep breath, finally calming down. "I can?" I asked.

He nodded toward the girls who had just been taunting me outside. "Don't let them get you nervous. You're prettier, smarter, and way cooler than all of them."

He grabbed a couple of sodas from an ice-filled bucket and handed me one. "So, you're Gen's cover story for tonight," he said as we pulled open the pop-tops. "That's usually my job."

"Why is it your job?" I asked.

"Being Gen's brother isn't easy," he answered.

"She's your sister?" I cried. I'd never suspected it!

He nodded. "Yeah."

Then I realized something even more surprising. "You're Tina's son?"

"Is that so hard to believe?" he asked, sounding offended.

"I just thought . . . uh . . . wow . . ." I didn't know how to tell him what I thought without insulting him even more than I already had.

"You thought I was the help," he supplied, saying it for me. "Well, I kind of am. Gen skates and I fix stuff. That rink was a pit when Mom bought it with her divorce money. I helped her bring it back. I did all the repair work, painting, the Zamboni." He smiled as he mentioned the Zamboni. "That's my favorite part. Ever since I was a kid I loved to take things apart and put them back together."

"That's your *calling*," I commented.

"Calling?" he asked.

"The thing you were born to do," I explained.

"Yeah, I guess it is," he said, seeming pleased with the idea. "It's funny to think of myself as having a calling. Gen is the one with the talent. In our family the focus has always been on getting Gen to the Nationals."

"Just because you don't skate, you don't think you have any talent?" I asked him. "Don't you think you're worth something, too?"

"I don't know," he admitted. "Am I?"

"I think you are," I told him.

He looked at me and seemed to absorb my words slowly, thinking about them. He suddenly seemed embarrassed to be talking about himself in such a personal way. "So, for you, your calling is the science stuff, I suppose," he said, shifting the focus to me.

I hesitated a moment before agreeing with that. "Right, I guess so," I replied, but to my surprise I realized I was no longer sure my answer was true. I had to admit to myself that, deep down, I had doubts.

Was my calling science—or was it skating?

Chapter 10

*T*iffany, Nikki, and Gen were so excited about the ways I was improving their moves with my physics calculations that they were constantly coming to me with new questions. In school, I was always with them talking about our workouts.

I tried to include Ann in all these skating conversations we were having in the hallways and at lunch, but it was hard for her to follow all the technical skating terms we used. I could tell she felt left out and I hoped she understood. Competitive figure skating was so thrilling to me that I just couldn't get enough of it.

When I wasn't discussing skating with Gen, Tiffany, and Nikki, I was at the rink skating. If I wasn't there, I was at the ballet studio learning to dance. Tiffany's parents were paying for those lessons in exchange for my helping Tiffany perfect her skating.

The bad thing was that all of this practice, and

learning, and teaching was exhausting me. I could barely keep my eyes open in class.

What made it even more of a strain was the fact that I was trying to do it all without Mom finding out. I convinced myself that I wasn't lying to her; I was simply keeping part of my life private.

In my heart I knew it was the same as lying, but I also knew she wouldn't understand and she definitely wouldn't approve. To Mom, academics were more important than anything. She'd feel like I was betraying her, turning my back on all the plans we'd made—the plans for my future as a superbrain achiever at some prestigious university, preferably Harvard.

It all came to a head late one afternoon when I came dragging in, completely exhausted, from a ballet lesson at the dance studio and then a workout session at the rink after school.

She sat on the couch, obviously waiting for me. "Where have you been?" she demanded.

"Stayed late at school," I replied. "You know, the tutoring thing." I'd made up a story about tutoring a kid in science. It was another half truth. I really was helping a guy in my physics class, except that Mr. Bast was letting me do it at the end of physics lab.

"Why are you doing this?" Mom asked. "This kid is obviously the dumbest kid on the planet. Tutoring him is taking up every spare second of your life."

"Mom, it looks good on my college application. Ann's doing it, too," I said.

"Ann was with you just now?" Mom asked.

"Yes," I told her, a total lie. "We were together just five minutes ago."

Mom stared with narrowed eyes. Alarm bells rang in my head. Her hurt, angry expression immediately told me my lie about Ann had given me away. "Ann just now called for you," she informed me.

I bit my lip. What could I possibly say now? I'd been busted, caught in a lie.

"What's going on?" Mom asked me. Her voice was gentle but firm.

"Mo-om," I pleaded softly. I was so tired that I didn't have the energy to even try to wiggle my way out of this mess.

"And since when do you get a C on a test?" she added. "I saw it in your room. I wasn't snooping but the test paper was right there on your desk. Is there something going on with you?"

"No!" I insisted.

"Is this a belated rebellion?" she probed. "When you got past fourteen, I relaxed. Maybe I shouldn't have relaxed." Then a new thought came to her. "Is it a boy?"

"Mo-om," I wailed. "No!"

"Sorry, I'm sorry," she said. "You do know what's at stake with your grades right now, don't you?"

"I know," I assured her wearily. "I feel bad about the C but could we just . . . *give it a rest!*" I didn't want to sound angry or impatient with Mom, but I felt so frazzled that it just came out that way.

Tears rushed to my eyes and I had to get out of there before they overflowed. If Mom saw me crying she'd never let me go until she had the truth. I started to run past her, but she reached up and grabbed my backpack to keep me from leaving. "Honey," she began to say as she unintentionally pulled the backpack from my shoulders and its contents spilled onto the floor.

My skates and Tina's flame-red skating outfit lay at her feet. Slowly she picked up the skating outfit.

I couldn't meet her eyes. I was ashamed of having lied, but even more than that, I was terrified that she'd insist I stop skating.

I went to my room and took a nap. Mom and I didn't speak again until dinner that night. We were halfway through the meal before Mom broke the silence first. "You can't hold all of this down!" she blurted all of a sudden. "Something's got to give! Do you want that something to be Harvard?"

It was definitely time to be honest with her. "Mom, I want to compete in the Regionals!" I revealed.

"Why?" she cried fiercely. "What do you gain by this?"

I dropped my eyes to my plate. How could I explain this to her when I didn't fully understand it myself? It wasn't rational, it was about the feeling I had when I skated. It was the exhilaration of landing a jump, the total, soaring joy of flying through the air and coming down cleanly.

All my life, I'd been a timid, brainy, sensible girl. But out on the rink, for the first time ever, I felt beautiful and magical and special.

I looked up at her. "I'm good, Mom," I told her.

"I know you have a flair for it," she began.

"It's not a flair!" I said heatedly. "I'm *really* good!"

Mom jumped up from the table, horrified by my words. Her hands clutched her head as though I'd given her a terrible headache. "So, what are you saying?" she demanded to know. "Do you want to just blow off our whole plan for you—chuck this scholarship and become a professional athlete?"

I had to hold my ground with her. This was something I really wanted with all my heart. If I backed down now, I'd lose everything I'd worked so hard for. "I can't stop thinking about it," I told her.

She sat back down and leaned across the table toward me. "Casey, what's the shelf life for a skater— eight years? So maybe you get a few medallions and if you're really, really lucky you get to wave from some *float* at some small-town parade! And then you'll spend a few years touring with 'Has-Beens On Ice!' After that—it's all over."

This time I couldn't stop the tears in my eyes from spilling over. "I love it, Mom," I said. "And I can't give it up."

Chapter 11

I continued to work with Gen, Nikki, and Tiffany on their skating while I trained and studied ballet. And even though Mom didn't stop me from training, she had no wish to see me skate, either. It was as if she simply didn't want to know anything about it.

That was why, when the big day came—the day I was to compete in the Regionals—Mom didn't even get out of bed to wish me luck. It was dawn when I rode my bike down to the Harwood Rink and got into a van along with Gen, Tiffany, and Nikki. All the parents and coaches, including Tina, were there, too, and Teddy drove.

It took us several hours to reach the Westerly Ice Rink, where the competition was being held. Nikki and her mother bragged the whole way about all the corporate sponsorships and "Jumping Shrimp" marketing opportunities that would be coming Nikki's way. Tiffany's parents tried to outdo Nikki's mom, claiming Tiffany would win even better deals.

Tina was mostly quiet. She closed her eyes and listened to the classical music she insisted on playing.

Gen and I sat together. She passed the time by giving me advice and telling me about all the ways skaters tried to gain a psychological edge by playing "mind games" on the other skaters.

"Watch this," she said. She turned around in her seat and spoke to Nikki. "Hey, Nik, everybody says you and me are going to pick up first and second today."

Nikki made a face at Gen, not buying it. "Nice try," she scoffed.

"What was *that* all about?" I asked Gen.

"It was a classic psych-out," she explained. "It softens up the competition, sets them up to think they don't have to go all out to win. Don't ever fall for it."

"Got it," I said.

"And no matter what happens in the short program, even if you tank," Gen went on, "you just keep telling yourself it's only a third of the score. Never freak until after the long program."

"Freak after long," I said, making a mental note. "Okay."

Gen sighed and shook her head. "I can't believe I'm giving away trade secrets," she said. To be honest, I could hardly believe it, either. I guessed it was a pretty good sign that we were really becoming friends.

We finally arrived at the Westerly Rink and entered

through the locker room. It was a big space full of lockers, ballet mirrors, and gym mats. About a dozen girls between the ages of about twelve and seventeen were already busy stretching and walking through their programs with sneakers on.

Gen took my arm and nodded toward a girl wearing headphones. She had a punk sort of look with lots of piercings. From the way she threw her head back and forth, I guessed she was listening to some kind of hard rock through those headphones. In my opinion, she was a little scary-looking. "That's Zoey Bloch," Gen whispered to me, "also known as Skate Thief."

Zoey turned and glowered at Nikki, who was right behind us. "Hmm. It's the leaping lizard," she sneered as she pushed her headphones off her ears and onto her neck.

"Jumping Shrimp," Nikki corrected her icily.

Zoey's lip curled into a contemptuous grin. "Like *that's* a step up."

"Don't get any closer to her, Nikki," Gen put in. "You don't want to lose your skates."

Zoey snorted with derision. "Like I'd need to steal her skates to win this thing—or some lame computer program, either."

I turned toward Gen. "How'd she know about that?" I asked.

"Her coach is Rasputin," Gen replied in a voice loud enough for Zoey to hear.

"Eat it, Harwood," Zoey snarled.

"Blow it out your—" Gen didn't get to finish because Tina swooped in and guided Gen away from the brewing fight. I couldn't hear what Tina was saying to Gen, but I guessed she was telling her not to let herself be distracted by Zoey.

Since I had no coach to tell me to stay focused, I told myself. I found a locker and changed into the hand-me-down red skating dress Tina had given me.

I was lacing my skates when Zoey came up and stood by the locker next to mine. I turned away, trying to pretend I hadn't noticed her. "So you're the one without the coach," she said.

Once she spoke, I couldn't just ignore her, so I turned in her direction. She'd changed into her skating outfit, a low-cut black dress that went with her hard, tough look. "Heard you're pretty good," she said. "Why'd you start so late?"

I blew her off with a flip remark. "I lost my watch," I replied, just wanting her to go away.

She took a step back. "Hey, I just wanted to wish you luck," she said, insulted. "It's not easy going out there your first time."

I felt bad. She hadn't done anything to me and I shouldn't have been so rude. "Thanks," I said.

"You just gotta keep focused and be impressive," she advised me. "Set the groundwork for next year."

"*Next* year?" I asked. Why couldn't I win *this* year?

"There's no way you're gonna place this year," she went on. "The judges have already ranked this thing in their minds. The skate's just a show for the fans."

I narrowed my eyes suspiciously. Could what she was saying be true?

"Nobody says it's fair," she continued. "They just don't know you." She glanced down at my old beat-up skates. "Nice skates," she said, tossing the remark over her shoulder as she walked away.

I'd almost forgotten what a mess my skates were, or maybe I'd just chosen to block it out of my mind. I wiggled my ankle. The skate's boot offered almost no support. The sight of the skates just pointed out how ridiculous this whole idea of mine was. How did I ever expect to compete against these girls with their expensive coaches and gorgeous, professional skates?

"Another classic psych-out," Gen said, coming up alongside me. "I heard what she said. It was the old 'You've already lost so why bother trying?' It's an old routine."

I sure had a lot to learn about all the dirty tricks that went on at these events.

Gen stepped back and looked me over a moment before speaking again. "Look, don't get offended, but I just want to ask you a little question."

"What?" I asked.

"Haven't you ever heard of eyeliner?"

Of course I'd heard of eyeliner. I just didn't wear it. What did she mean by that?

"This is your big moment," Gen continued. "Don't you want everyone to see your face?" She stepped away and returned in half a minute with her makeup bag, holding it up to me.

I suddenly got it. She was saying that I needed to wear makeup and she was offering to apply it for me. Nodding that it was okay, I followed her into the warm-up room and sat down in front of a mirror.

She turned the swivel chair to face her. I closed my eyes as she worked, deftly applying the makeup. The makeup she wore always looked great, so I figured she'd do a good job. Just the same, I was more than a little nervous. I'd never worn makeup and couldn't imagine myself in it. What if I came out looking like a kid playing dress-up with a grown-up's makeup?

Finally, she stopped working. I opened my eyes as she spun me around to face the mirror.

Was it really my face I was seeing? I hardly recognized myself. "I'm . . ."

"Yeah," Gen said. "The P word—you can say it."

But I *couldn't* say anything. I was literally speechless. I *was* pretty.

Gen looked at my image in the mirror and smiled. "Now, hands off Brian," she teased playfully. "He's mine. But you can have Teddy."

I allowed myself a shaky smile. I loved the new way I looked and the idea that Teddy might like it, too, suddenly made me very happy.

It was finally time for the first event, the Ladies Short Program. I stood behind the boards watching, nervously awaiting my turn to skate.

Zoey Bloch was the first skater out. Heavy-metal music blasted the rink to life as she kicked into a daredevil aerial followed by fast and furious footwork. Her performance was incredibly dynamic and done in a style all her own. I looked to the judges to see their reaction to Zoey's skating. Some of them looked very impressed while others seemed a little turned off by the hard-rock music.

Nikki was the next to skate. She nailed an amazing triple salchow and then quickly went into the flying sit spin, which was great, thanks in part to my computer analysis. The crowd applauded loudly and the judges nodded as they wrote their scores.

Tiffany skated next. I watched anxiously, realizing that she was leaning too far forward on her triple toe loop. I hoped she could somehow hang on, but she lost her footing and fell! The crowd groaned and I noticed her father stiffen with displeasure. Like a true professional, Tiffany got up and kept skating, but I knew the fall would hurt her score.

When it was Gen's turn, she did a double lutz and moved into a perfect sit spin. Everyone cheered when she landed an amazing double axel. At the end of the routine she spun so fast she was a blur before coming to a dramatic stop.

She should have been overjoyed, but, to me, she seemed oddly emotionless as she skated off the ice. Tina met her at the boards. "Okay, we're in," she said. "You're definitely in the top four."

"You're going to the Sectionals!" Teddy cheered, squeezing her shoulders. She was breathing hard, still recovering from the exertion of her routine.

I was next. The moment had finally come.

Teddy caught my eye and shot me an encouraging smile. Gen smiled at me, too. I nodded back to them as I skated out onto the ice.

"Our next skater is Casey Carlyle from Millbrook, Connecticut," the announcer boomed over the public address system.

I reached the center of the ice and looked into

the bleachers at the crowd. They were chatting and laughing. Some were out of their seats heading to the bathroom or the snack bar. They were definitely not breathless with anticipation at the idea of my upcoming performance.

A glance at the judges told me they were equally unexcited about seeing me skate. One judge checked her watch. Another gazed absently at his score sheet. Not one of them seemed to be interested in the least in what I was preparing to do.

Focus! I commanded myself. Letting myself get all upset that the crowd wasn't eager to see me wasn't going to help anything. Why should they be eager? As Zoey had said, they didn't know me—not yet.

I took a deep breath to steady my nerves. My program music began and I glided into my first jump—a double flip. Right away I knew that my launch was a bit stiff. As I came down, my right ankle gave out, throwing me off balance. I was pretty sure that the bad condition of my skates was partly to blame for my not landing the jump.

I remembered how Tiffany got up after falling and it was what I had to do, also. Getting back into my routine, I picked up speed until I felt ready to launch my double axel. The jump was high and I landed it cleanly.

Impressed *Oohs* and *Ahhs* followed the jump. Some

people starting clapping along with my music. I could just tell I'd caught their attention now.

The audience was energizing me and I suddenly felt more confident and ready to show everyone what I could do—what I *hoped* I could do. As the clapping grew louder I launched another jump—this time it was a jump I'd never attempted before, a triple-double combination.

I flew into the air, climbing higher and higher. There was not a single thought in my head. It was time for my body to use all the information it had learned these last months, all the timing and balance I'd trained into it.

The moment my blade touched the ice again, I knew it was going to come out all right. And it was! I skated out of the jump cleanly, my heart hammering.

The crowd's cheers roared in my ears!

Tears of pride and joy sprang to my eyes!

I'd gone beyond what even I'd thought I could do. As I skated off the ice I felt like I really had a shot at placing in the top four, which meant that in six months I would go on to the next event, the Sectionals. I just hoped the triple-double combination would offset my bad first jump.

It seemed like forever before we got the scores. I sat alone in the kiss-and-cry area and waited for the numbers to appear on the scoreboard. My technical scores were pretty good and my scores of artistry were even better.

Twelve other skaters had to perform before a judge posted our ranking on a bulletin board in the warm-up room. Nikki screamed ecstatically when she saw she'd placed in the number one spot. "You earned it, baby!" her mother said, hugging her.

Zoey Bloch was number two. "It's only the short program, shorty," she said to Nikki, making it sound like a threat.

Tiffany ranked third, but instead of being pleased that she'd placed, her father shot her a disappointed frown. "Dad, I'm still ranked," she pointed out.

"You're not first," he said grimly, walking away from her. I wondered how he could be so harsh with his own daughter. Tiffany was obviously crushed by his reaction. I'd been feeling a little bad about not having a parent there with me—but at that moment I considered that it might be a plus.

"Fourth," Gen said, reading her score.

"We'll take it," Tina commented.

I was right behind her—fifth. I'd come so close, but I hadn't placed.

My disappointment must have shown on my face because Gen came over and put her hand on my shoulder. "Come on—fifth, that's great!" she said kindly. "If you skate a clean program tonight, you can move up and knock me out of fourth."

"But fifth doesn't go to Sectionals," I reminded her.

"I'll take care of myself," she assured me, walking away. I couldn't imagine what she could be thinking. Maybe she thought we could both move up. Her words had made me think about the next event and wonder how I was going to get through it with my skates in such poor condition. I sat on a bench and as I started to unlace them I saw that they were more shabby-looking than ever. They'd really taken a beating in the short program.

Tina sat down beside me on the bench. I suppose she could see my concern about the skates. "Casey, you almost lost a boot out there," she said.

"I know," I admitted, pulling off the skate. "It's giving out."

"I think you'd better come with me," Tina said, getting up. I quickly pulled off the other skate and hurried to follow her. Together we walked down a long hallway until we arrived at the rink's Pro Shop.

Inside, Tina asked me my shoe size and then said something to the salesman. He disappeared into a back room. When he reappeared, he had a pair of skate boots in a box. Tina directed me to sit and the salesman put them on my feet. "How do they feel?" she asked.

"Great," I said. "But I can't accept these."

"You can work it off," she replied. "I really just can't stand to see you held back this way." She turned to the salesman, handing him her credit card. "And we'll need a pair of blades."

"I'll sharpen them right up," he told her.

I was overwhelmed by her kindness. I didn't know what to say but I needed to let her know how much I appreciated what she was doing. "Tina . . . I . . . I just can't believe—"

She held up her hand and cut me off. "No fawning."

"No," I agreed. "Just . . . thanks."

Not only were the skates beautiful, but they'd give me a real shot at placing in the long event that night. As I looked down at the glistening white skates, I really believed my dream was suddenly within my reach.

Chapter 12

There I was, poised at the center of the rink in my gleaming new skates, ready for my performance in the Junior Ladies Long Program to begin—ready as I'd ever be, anyway.

My music began and I started to skate, picking up speed in preparation for my first jump, a double axel. I took off, tucked in tight, and spun two and a half times.

Yes!

But when I touched down, I suddenly felt as if my feet were on fire and my ankles were being crushed. These new skates were stiff; the boots didn't bend or give at all!

The crowd gasped as I lost control of my landing, wobbling horribly. It was so painful that I couldn't believe it! It took all my willpower to hold on to the landing and not fall over completely.

Regaining my footing and composure, I continued.

To have any hope of completing my program I'd need to fight through the agony the skates were causing. Sucking in my breath, I put my head down and tried to concentrate on my next jump. It would be the most difficult one in the routine, the triple flip.

I dug my pick into the ice and the burning, crushing pain returned, worse than ever. It was so terrible it made me gasp, but I couldn't think about it!

I leapt into the air, grateful to be off my feet. I turned—one, two, three times! The searing pain returned as I came down, but it didn't matter. I'd stuck it—a perfect landing!

The crowd exploded with applause!

I smiled despite my tortured feet. The hardest part was over. All that was left was to survive the rest of the routine. Finally I skated off with the sounds of loud applause all around me. I should have been thrilled but I was in too much pain to enjoy the moment.

Alone again in the kiss-and-cry area, I immediately loosened my laces. Once again, my scores were okay. They seemed to be pretty close to Gen's scores and I couldn't figure out where either of us now ranked.

I'd been the last skater to perform and the ranking was posted in the locker room before I even had my skates off. Zoey Bloch had risen to first place. Nikki was second. Tiffany was still in third place, which sent her father storming off in an angry huff.

Gen screamed with delight when she saw she'd hung on to fourth place. She hugged Nikki and Tiffany. "We're going to the Sectionals!" she cried.

I watched them all sadly. I was still in fifth place, which meant I wasn't going anywhere.

Bitterly disappointed, I hobbled to a bench and began pulling off my skates. The pain was unbelievable as I slipped my foot out and I quickly saw the cause of it. My tights were covered in blood from the blisters that had formed on my feet.

Zoey was at a nearby locker changing into her street clothes and she turned when I groaned in pain. "Are those new?" she asked, nodding at my skates.

"Yeah," I answered.

"Are you crazy?" she cried. "You can't compete on new skates! They take a minimum of ten days to break in. Everybody knows that!"

I was confused. "But Tina didn't tell me—"

"You mean Tina whose robot daughter almost didn't make the Sectionals because of you?" Zoey sneered.

It took a minute for me to understand Zoey's meaning, but when it sunk in I felt sick to my stomach. Was she saying Tina had tricked me into wearing new skates so I wouldn't beat Gen out of the Sectionals?

"Typical Tina Harwood," Zoey continued. "This is just like what happened in Calgary."

Now I was even more confused. What was she talking about?

"You don't know anything, do you?" Zoey said, amused by my ignorance. "They kicked her out."

Zoey slung her backpack over her shoulder. "You may want to reconsider that no-coach thing," she said as she sauntered out of the room.

She had a good point. If I'd had a coach who was looking out for me, this wouldn't have happened.

I'd never felt so betrayed in my life! I was furious and hurt at the same time. I slipped out of the other skate, revealing an equally bloody mess.

Looking around, I spotted Gen, Teddy, and Tina all standing together. I was close to tears, but I wouldn't let them see me cry. Instead, I walked over and confronted Tina. "Are you happy about my feet?" I asked angrily.

Tina stayed cool. "I'm sorry, Casey, but your old skates were a mess."

"You bought her *new* skates?" Gen asked her mother in a voice filled with disbelief.

I didn't believe her innocent act! "Oh, like you didn't know?" I shouted.

"I didn't!" she cried.

Of course she'd known. I was sure of it now. How could I have thought Gen Harwood would want to be my friend? This was all just a setup to get me out of the way. And, in a way, Gen had even warned me, telling me skating was full of dirty tricks. "I am an idiot!" I said to Gen. "And you're a little horror!"

"Don't say that to her," Teddy defended his little sister.

"Oh, right," I sneered, "like you weren't part of this, too."

He stepped back as though I'd slapped him. "How could you think that?" he yelled.

"Because it's true!" I shouted right back at him. "Your whole family set me up!"

Gen and Teddy tried to look shocked, but Tina didn't even attempt to fake it. Her face was stony. She knew I'd figured it out.

I stared at them and shook my head sadly. "What kind of people are you?" I asked tearfully.

Hurrying into the hallway, I found a pay phone and called home. As soon as I heard Mom's voice, I started to sob. "Can you come and get me?" I asked through my tears. "I'm at the rink at Westerly. I want to come home."

Chapter 13

J'd never seen Mom so furious. "I guess a leopard never really changes its spots," she said as she drove me home.

When I asked her what she meant she told me that Tina had been thrown out of the Calgary Olympics because she had somehow injured another skater. "Everyone in town was gossiping about it when it first happened. I never got the details," she said. "I didn't mention it to you because I like to think everyone deserves a second chance. But, apparently, someone like Tina just can't change.

"At least now you can focus on your interview at Harvard next week," Mom said as she pulled into our driveway.

On Sunday I gazed out at the pond that was visible from my bedroom window and thought about how I used to love skating on it when I was a kid. Back then

I slid around on the ice for the pure joy of it. There were no blistered feet, no nasty competitions full of betrayal, just the wonderful freedom of sailing along on the ice.

Monday came too quickly and I had to go back to school. I dreaded the prospect of seeing Gen there. I was hoping to just ignore her because I really wanted to forget I'd ever even seen her, Tina, Teddy, or a pair of ice skates. But she caught up to me as I walked to physics class.

"Go away," I told her, quickening my pace.

"I didn't know about it," she insisted, grabbing my arm. "And there's something you have to know."

I stopped and faced her. "What could you possibly have to tell me that I would want to hear?" I asked.

"I'm done with skating," she said. "I told my mother yesterday. As you can guess, she was majorly freaked, but this has been coming for a long time. I've had to face the truth. I just don't have the talent that it takes."

This was unbelievable—Gen Harwood quitting skating? "How can you quit after all the work you've put in?" I asked.

"I want to quit," she insisted. "I want to stop missing school because I'm too busy practicing my skating. I want to go to the Homecoming Dance and I want to go with Brian. And I want to stop feeling like an idiot for flunking math because I don't have time to learn it.

I want to eat a big, fat, greasy hamburger with double fries and to finally know the shows on TV that the other kids are talking about."

She really was serious and obviously she'd given it a lot of thought.

"If I drop out, you're ranked next," she added. "You can go to the Sectionals. It should be your slot anyway."

I shook my head. "No," I told her. "Thanks, Gen, but tomorrow's my Harvard interview. *That's* my slot. *That's* what I should be doing."

Gen shot me a doubtful look. "Are you sure about that?" she questioned.

I nodded, although I'd never been less sure of anything.

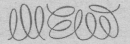

The next day we set out for Harvard very early in the morning. Once again, Mom had bought me one of her "serious" outfits. I tried not to worry about my geeky appearance as we walked across the campus, passing stately brick buildings with pillars in front.

"Look," Mom said, showing me her forearm. "I've got goose bumps."

I looked and she wasn't lying. Her arm was covered in tiny bumps. The idea of being here with me at

Harvard was so exciting to her. I wished I felt even a quarter of her excitement.

"It's just that it's so much like the brochure," she said as we stopped in front of the Harvard Admissions Office. We went inside and found the office of a man named Chip Healy. He welcomed us in, shaking our hands, and told us to sit in the leather armchairs in front of his wide desk.

He had a folder in front of him on the desk. He quickly scanned the pages and then looked up at me with a smile. "So, you're up for the Stoller Scholarship," he remarked. "This skating project you did for them is very ambitious."

"Well, I *was* able to prove some of my theories," I said.

He nodded, seeming genuinely interested. "Many scientists become their own guinea pig. Can you tell me how this depth of research affected your thinking?"

Wow! That was such a big question that I wasn't really sure how to answer. I had to say something, though, so I gave it my best try. "I guess . . . uh . . . what I learned was . . ." I began, trying to think fast while I stalled for time by talking slowly.

"What I learned was that physics really can explain a lot about a sport, like speed and balance and the arc of a spin. It just can't . . . it can't explain how skating makes you feel."

"And how is that?" Mr. Healy asked.

"There's a definite exhilaration," I began, still trying

to sound scholarly and scientific. "I found it quite thrilling. It was a rewarding project and the guinea pig angle added a dimension I . . . uh . . . hadn't anticipated."

I stared at him a moment, as I listened to my own words on a sort of mental instant replay. I knew this was all wrong. It wasn't what I really wanted to say. I couldn't pretend to be distant and analytical about something I felt so passionate about. I didn't want to spend my time *analyzing* skating—I WANTED TO SKATE!

"I don't think I can come here," I blurted, suddenly standing. "I'm sorry I wasted your time. I'm sorry."

The next day, I sat down beside Ann in the lunchroom. "Are you talking to me?" I asked.

"I'm not the one who stopped talking," she said coolly, not looking at me as she ate her sandwich.

That was a little unfair, I thought. I hadn't stopped talking to her, I was just busy. "If I could've made more time for you—"

"You would've," she cut me off. "Yeah, yeah."

There was silence between us. What could I really say? In a way, I *had* taken our friendship for granted these past months—but that was because I'd assumed Ann and I were such good friends that a little time apart wouldn't kill the friendship.

"I heard you blew off Harvard," she said after a few more minutes of silence.

She must have heard that from her mother, who sometimes talks to my mom. Mom had been totally freaked by what I did at Harvard. At least, at first she was. Then, later, she cooled down, but I could tell she was extremely disappointed in me.

"I don't have the support of a single human being," I told Ann, "but I still want to go to the Sectionals."

She stared at me with the same amazed lack of understanding as Mom. "So, that's everything now?" she asked.

"I wish it wasn't," I admitted. "Ann, I don't know what—"

She clamped her hand down on my wrist, squeezing slightly. "Don't," she insisted. "Don't look to me for help. I'm still totally mad at you. I don't even know if we're friends anymore. You've got your new friends to talk to."

"I don't," I told her. "I can't go to the rink."

Ann looked at me, not understanding. "So, how are you going to practice?" she asked.

I didn't know.

For someone who was supposed to be a brain, I'd been pretty stupid. I hadn't even thought of that.

How could I even think of going to the Sectionals if I had nowhere to practice?

Chapter 14

It was where I'd first learned to skate. What better place to practice than the pond behind my house? I bundled up in a sweater and jeans, grabbed my boom box, and headed out to the pond.

I'd also taken the new skates Tina had used to trick me. I hated the sight of them and the painful memories they brought. But my old skates were useless and the new ones were the only skates I would have to wear in the Sectionals. I had to break them in.

As I stepped out onto the ice in the new skates, my feet once again burned. This time, though, I'd taped them with bandages at the sensitive spots and worn the thickest socks I could get into the skates. I began to skate and I was glad to discover that the discomfort was bearable.

All the months I'd spent skating at the Harwood Rink had made me forget something about skating on a frozen pond.

Pond ice is bumpy.

Every time I built up speed, I stumbled on little nubs of rough ice. When I landed a jump, I'd turn and nearly fall on a choppy patch.

I was determined to make it work, though. I'd skated through the pain of those awful new skates and I could skate past a few bumps. Pushing off the ice, I jumped a huge triple, gaining more height than ever before. I came down clean, and stumbled on some ridges of ice, coming down hard on my right side.

It felt like ages before I stopped sliding across the pond. My knee ached and so did my elbow. I was pretty certain they'd be black and blue in a few hours, although I didn't think I'd broken anything.

Getting onto my knees, I got up and went to sit on a nearby fallen log. I pushed my face into a knot, struggling not to cry. I wanted to be finished with tears.

With my eyes squeezed shut, I became aware of a low hum. Was the boom box making the sound? Looking over to check it, I saw that the sound wasn't coming from the boom box but from a huge machine that was slowly rising over a nearby hill.

At first, I didn't even know what I was looking at. And then suddenly I realized what it was.

It was a Zamboni—and Teddy was driving it!

I stood and watched as he steered it toward me.

He stopped at the edge of the pond. "How did you know?" I asked, walking over to meet him.

He grinned, clearly pleased at the amazed expression on my face. "I didn't think you'd just give up," he explained, "which meant you'd be out here bumping it out."

This was amazing!

"Teddy," I began. "I've been trying to find some way to apologize to you for the things I said."

"I've got some ideas about how you can do that," he said with a smile.

From the heat in my cheeks, I could tell I was blushing. I hoped he'd think it was just the cold.

He moved the Zamboni onto the pond. "Do you like your ice medium smooth or glassy?" he asked as he drove it forward.

When Teddy finished with the pond it was a glistening thing of beauty. If I'd closed my eyes as I sailed out onto it, I could have imagined I was back at the rink.

He came down from the Zamboni seat as I performed my routine for him. With the ice smoothed out, nothing could stop me. When I'd spun to a finish, I smiled at him, feeling like I'd never stop smiling.

He came out onto the ice beside me, still clapping. "I'm usually so shy," I admitted. "How come I can do a whole performance in front of you?" I asked.

"You let people see you when you skate," he said, looking into my eyes.

I looked down, suddenly feeling very shy, but he gently lifted my chin with his finger. "Don't worry," he said. "It's a nice view."

He leaned in toward me and, for a second, I thought we were about to kiss. But the sound of an approaching car made us jump apart. "Is that your mom?" he asked.

I shook my head. Mom's car doesn't have a muffler. We went around the side of the house and saw Tina getting out of her car in my driveway. "What's she doing here?" I asked.

"I know why," Teddy said nervously. He stepped forward, approaching his mother. "Mom, look," he began, "I took the Zamboni. I know that was way wrong and probably illegal, but I kept off the main roads. I only wanted to help Casey out because I thought *somebody* owed her."

It must have been hard for him to stand up to his mother like that, but he continued. "And, you know, none of this would have happened if this sport weren't filled with nut jobs!"

"I'm not here about the Zamboni," Tina said calmly.

"You're not?" Teddy cried, shocked.

"Just make sure it gets back in one piece," she insisted.

"I will. No sweat," he assured her.

"I came to talk to Casey," Tina said, looking at me. "I want to train you for the Sectionals."

"What?" I asked with disbelief. "Are you crazy?"

Her eyes held mine as she spoke, appearing to be completely serious. "Teddy can smooth out the ice all he wants, but he can't smooth out your skating—which, if he's honest, he'll tell you is all over the place. Not a chance!"

I couldn't believe her nerve!

I turned to Teddy, wanting to see how he was taking this from his mother. To my surprise, he didn't seem angry with her. "She's right, Case," he said. "You can't win."

"Not without me," Tina added.

Teddy walked off toward the Zamboni, leaving me alone with Tina. For a moment, we just looked at each other. Then I asked her what had happened at Calgary. I had to know if the thing Mom had told me was true and if I could trust her.

"I had an unfortunate warm-up before my short program. I collided with another skater and she got hurt," she told me. "There was talk because I'd been chasing her scores for years but no one could prove a thing."

"But was it on purpose?" I insisted on knowing.

Tina's expression grew very hard, even for Tina.

"Look, I paid my dues," she said defensively. "They threw me out and by the time they considered reinstating me, I was twenty-six and it was too late."

As much as I mistrusted Tina, at that moment I felt a twinge of sympathy for her. I knew how it felt to have your dreams swept away.

"There's not a day that goes by that I don't wish I could relive that moment and do it differently," Tina added.

"Are you really sorry?" I pressed her. "Or do you just want me to think you are so I'll train with you?"

"I'm not going to beg," she replied.

"I'll think about it," I said. That was for sure! I knew I wouldn't be able to think about anything else until I'd decided.

Chapter 15

"*T*hat you might even consider letting that woman back into . . ." Mom shouted, but she was so furious that she couldn't finish her sentence. She just paced, quaking with anger, back and forth across the kitchen floor.

But I knew from my lessons and from watching Gen train that Tina was an awesome coach. "I don't have to like her, or trust her," I said.

"No! You just have to spend all your time with her!" Mom exploded.

"I'm not going to turn into her," I insisted.

"She's *already* rubbed off on you!" Mom said.

My jaw fell in shocked astonishment. How could she say that? "That's not true!" I objected.

"Oh?" Mom replied, raising her eyebrows skeptically. She waved her hand, pointing at me. "Where did this makeup come from?" she challenged. "And this hair? And that shirt? I didn't buy you that."

It was true that ever since Gen worked her mini makeover on me at the Regionals, I'd changed my appearance. I had liked the way I looked that day and I wanted to keep it up. It wasn't because of Tina, though. "Mom, that has nothing to do with—" I began to explain.

But Mom cut me short. "I think you want to be exactly like her!"

"Why are you jealous of her?" I asked.

Mom stopped pacing, stunned by my accusation. Slowly, she sat down at the kitchen table. "Well . . . " she began with a thoughtful look on her face. "I guess no matter how old we get . . . the rest of us will always still hate the Prom Queen."

One of the things I love about my mom is that even at the worst of times, she can still find something sort of funny to say. I really did understand how she felt. She only wanted to protect me, just like she'd been doing her whole life. "You know it's always going to be the Casey-and-Mom show," I said.

"Do I?" she asked. "Then what have we been working toward all these years?" Her eyes pleaded with me to take her words to heart. "The time to go to school is now!"

"I will go," I promised. "Later."

"When?!" Mom demanded impatiently. "Do you plan to go at night after your crummy day job, when you're thirty-five years old and scared out of your wits that you can't even feed your kid?"

I realized she was talking about her own experience. "I know it was hard for you," I said.

I understood *her* feelings but I had to make her see how *I* felt. "If you could only just come to the rink and see what I'm doing," I suggested. "You haven't come, not once."

Mom raised her hands, as if to stop my words from reaching her. "Don't ask me. I can't." She stood up and began to walk away.

"Come with me!" I insisted. "Right now!" She stopped walking and turned to face me. "Mom, come watch me skate," I pleaded. "And then tell me I should stop. *Please.* Come now!"

Mom picked up her purse from the table. "I have a class," she said and walked out of the kitchen.

I leaned back in my kitchen chair and sighed. It seemed I'd made up my mind. I was going to go for the Sectionals and Tina Harwood would be my coach. Getting up, I walked to the kitchen phone, picked it up, and pressed in Tina's office number at the rink.

My very first session was early the next morning. I went down to the rink by myself and when I arrived,

I found Gen in the bleachers and sat beside her. She was watching Tina skate out on the ice.

Tina was in the middle of doing an amazing spiral. "She doesn't do it very much anymore," Gen said.

"She must have been great," I commented, truly impressed.

"Whether you like it or not," Gen said, "she's the best."

Tina spun to a stop and noticed me sitting in the bleachers. "When I say six-thirty, I do not mean six-thirty-three!" she barked.

Gen turned to me with a shrug. "It's your torture now. Why am I even out of bed?"

Teddy appeared at the top of the stairs. "Hey, Case—" he called, hurrying down toward me.

"And NO distractions!" Tina shouted. Teddy and I looked at each other, wishing we could have just a minute together. "Both of you know exactly what I'm talking about!" she added.

"Yeah. I know," Teddy said with a resigned sigh.

"What?" I asked him. "She dictates both of our social lives?"

He nodded. "If you want to win, then yeah."

I turned toward Tina. Maybe this wasn't such a good idea, after all. I felt a strong urge to tell her just where to get off. I didn't owe her anything.

But, looking back at Teddy, I understood what he

was telling me. I *did* want to win. Tina was my best, and maybe *only,* chance of doing that.

So I kept my mouth shut and took out my skates as Teddy walked back up the stairs.

I'd put in so many hours of practice that I couldn't even count them; but now, months after I'd begun to train with Tina, I was finally at the Sectionals, held in the Liberty Gardens Arena.

As I did my warm-up out on the ice with the other contestants, I looked up to the announcer's booth high above me. In it sat two of my skating idols—Turner Banks and Michelle Kwan. I could hear their words over the public address system.

"Welcome to ESPN's live coverage of the New England Regional Ladies Short Program," Turner Banks announced. "I've got to say, from the looks of the practice session I'm seeing down on the ice right now, these ladies are definitely fired up!"

"That's right, Turner," Michelle Kwan agreed. "They have come to compete!"

Nikki, who skated nearby, was definitely fired up. She was sticking triple jump after triple jump. A cheering section of fans waved their plush stuffed shrimp dolls and held signs that read: GO NIKKI! and JUMPING SHRIMP RULES! Nikki waved to them like a real champion, too.

The skater Chantal DeGroat was there, marking out her routine with cautious precision. Her shiny skating outfit sparkled against her dark skin as she moved slowly and gracefully.

Turner Banks continued to talk over the PA system. "Some of you might remember the controversy surrounding last year's competition, when first-place contender Chantal DeGroat's skate disappeared from her locker right before the long program. Because of that, she skated poorly and fell out of medal contention, leaving rock 'n' roll bad girl Zoey Bloch to skate away with the gold." I remembered that Gen had told me she thought Zoey Bloch was the one who had stolen Chantal DeGroat's skate.

Zoey grinned as she practiced her footwork not far from me. At the mention of her name, she skated to the boards and raised her arms to the crowd, pumping up the excitement. A rowdy group of punky fans roared their support.

While the others warmed up, I was also concentrating on my routine. After all the months of practice, my skates no longer hurt. In fact, when they were on they felt so natural they were like a part of my foot.

My mind was on my footwork when another skater, one I didn't know, whooshed past, going backwards. I darted out of her path just in time to avoid a collision. She'd been way too close.

Instinctively, I looked to Tina. Had she seen that? She had, and nodded at me. Her look said: *Be careful out there.*

Glancing into the bleachers, I saw that I had my own small fan section. Gen and Ann sat together, talking, and even smiling at each other. It would be great if my two best friends became friends with each other.

Finally it was time for the competition to begin. We skated off the ice and headed for the warm-up room where we could watch the performances in the rink on a closed-circuit TV.

Zoey skated first to a hard-rock song. "This girl skates all out," Turner Banks commented, "and the crowd is just rockin' out!" It was true. She was dynamite and the crowd exploded with applause when she landed a killer double lutz.

Tiffany was the next to skate. "When Tiffany is on, she's probably the most graceful skater in this entire competition," Michelle Kwan remarked to the crowd and the ESPN audience. "And she is definitely on today," she added as Tiffany went into an incredible spin.

Chantal DeGroat stunned the audience next with an awesome triple jump. "She wants that gold!" Turner Banks said enthusiastically.

I stood behind the boards while Nikki skated. I was up right after her and it took all the self-discipline I had to keep breathing and not become a jumble of panicked nerves. To distract myself, I tried to concentrate on watching Nikki perform.

Nikki more than earned her reputation as the Jumping Shrimp. "This little dynamo has been landing massive jumps lately," Turner Banks noted as Nikki launched a triple toe loop high into the air, came down, and went right into some complicated footwork.

She skated off the ice and I skated on. "The word *newcomer* doesn't even begin to describe Casey Carlyle," Turner Banks told the crowd as I headed for the center of the rink.

"She's never performed in *any* skating competition *anywhere* until this season," Michelle Kwan added. "She's definitely a skater to keep your eye on."

I forced my lips into a nervous smile as my music began. I could hardly think but I had the feeling my routine was going well. I heard applause when I landed a clean triple-double combination. There was more clapping when I did my spin. I didn't fall or even wobble.

I couldn't tell how my performance had compared to the others, but I skated off happy, feeling I'd done the best I could. I would just have to wait to find out if it had been good enough.

That moment soon came while Tina and I waited in the kiss-and-cry area.

I was thrilled to get 4.9s and 5.2s. There was even one 5.3. "And one four-point-seven," Tina pointed out. Although I was all smiles, she seemed concerned. "You're in the game, that's all," she said.

I unlaced my skates and pulled them off. Tina tossed them in a locker and went to lock them up, only to discover that there was no lock. "The security in here is as lousy as ever," she muttered as she slammed the locker door shut.

All the skaters gathered in the lounge to hear Turner Banks announce how we'd all placed. Zoey was first, Nikki was second—and I was third!

I jumped up, ecstatic. I'd actually placed at the Sectionals! It was too good to be true!

Gen rushed into the lounge and hugged me. "You pulled it out, girl!" she cried.

"It's only the short program," I said, reminding her of what she'd told me.

"I lied," she admitted, laughing. "If you mess up the short program, you can never win!"

I laughed with her. This was so great. If only Mom

had been there to see this, everything would have been perfect. I tried not to think about her not being there, though. Tonight was the long program. I couldn't let anything distract me from skating the best long program I'd ever skated.

Chapter 16

"Just keep visualizing yourself landing a perfect triple loop," Gen advised me as we entered the locker room for the long program. "You feel the blade hitting at the exact right angle, and you know you're going to stick it."

I nodded while pulling open the locker I'd seen Tina toss my skates into.

I blinked, staring into the empty locker. At first, my brain couldn't make sense of what I was seeing—or, I should say, of what I *wasn't* seeing! But then it hit me and it hit me hard.

MY SKATES WERE GONE!

My breaths became short and fast as panic overwhelmed me. Gen glanced into the empty locker and instantly understood the problem. "They can't be far. We'll find them," she assured me, pulling open locker after locker.

In an instant, the other skaters in the room became

aware of what had happened. Everyone turned suspicious eyes toward Zoey Bloch. "What are you freaks looking at?" she snapped.

Gen took a threatening step toward her. "Give them back, Zoey!" she demanded.

"Back off, Harwood," Zoey growled. "I'll mess you up!"

Gen squared her shoulders and kept advancing on Zoey. "I don't care if you do. I'm not skating, but you are!"

Gen's words scared Zoey, who backed away. At that moment, Tina stepped between the two of them. "Stop it, Gen," she said. "She didn't do it."

Everyone was now staring at Tina. "She's not threatened by you," she explained to me. "The question is . . . who here is threatened the most?"

Tina wheeled around to face Nikki's mother and reached into her oversized bag. In a second, she had pulled out my skates!

Nikki's mom pretended to be shocked. "I don't know how those could've—"

"Can it, Maureen," Tina said, cutting her off sharply. "You're talking to a pro."

It was hard not to grin at the mortified look on Nikki's mother's face. Tina had sliced her to ribbons with a few words.

"Tina, how did you know?" I asked her.

"I know how far parents in this sport will go," she replied. As she said these words, she looked at Gen rather than at me. I think Gen knew what I knew—that this was as close to an apology as she was ever going to get from Tina. Judging from the soft smile on Gen's face, I guess it was enough for her.

Tina then turned her attention to me. "Lace up," she commanded.

"But what happens to Nikki?" I asked.

"She'll be disqualified," Tina told me in a matter-of-fact tone.

Nikki stepped forward. "But I didn't know anything about it!" she objected dramatically. Although she was a terrific skater, she wasn't much of an actress. I'd never seen a worse performance.

"That's true, Tina," Nikki's mother agreed. "She didn't know." I saw where Nikki had gotten her lack of acting talent from. What phonies!

Tina shook her head. "Sorry. I'm making a report."

"Don't," I said. All eyes turned to me, shocked. "Don't," I repeated. "I want to skate her, fair and square." I'd never know how good I really was if I eliminated one of my closest competitors on a technicality. Nikki probably deserved to be disqualified—I didn't believe she wasn't in on this for a second—but

I also deserved the chance to test myself against her in this event.

Tina regarded me thoughtfully. "Well . . ." she considered. "There's something to be said for avoiding a scandal." She turned to Nikki. "You just came this close to a boxing career," she told her.

I avoided looking at Nikki or her mother as I put on my skates. The event began and I gazed up at the closed-circuit TV. "From New York, New York, Miss Emma Flanders," Turner Banks announced as the first skater sailed out onto the ice.

Tina sat alongside me on the bench and held out her hand to me, offering me something. Looking down, I saw that she was giving me earplugs. "I forgot to tell you this during the short program, but I'm telling you now," she said. "You can lose the long program just sitting here if you don't prepare properly."

I stared at her, not understanding, as she pressed the earplugs into my hand. "Put these in," she insisted. "Believe me, you don't want to know what's going on out there. If a skater falls, you'll get overconfident. If she brings the crowd to its feet, you'll feel pressure. Don't watch the performances, don't hear them—stay in your head, loving your skate. No one else exists."

It sounded like it might be good advice, so I put in the earplugs. I turned my back on the TV and tried to block it all out. Tina had to tap me on the shoulder when it was almost my turn to skate.

With my earplugs still in, I stood behind the boards with my back turned to Nikki, my hands over my ears. One time the crowd cheered so loudly for her that I couldn't help but hear it.

Tina had been right—it was unnerving.

I suddenly wished my mother was in the audience. Of course it was great to have Ann and Gen there. I was pretty sure Teddy was out there somewhere, too, although Tina had probably put him under strict orders to stay away. But it wasn't the same as having Mom there. Mom and I had been a team for so long, it didn't seem right not to share this with her.

Gen came alongside me and I asked to use her cell phone to call Mom. I just wanted to hear her voice, but I only reached our answering machine.

I hadn't realized that Tina had come up behind me while I was calling. "This is not about her," she said in a surprisingly kind voice.

Nodding, I knew this was about *me* doing *my* best.

"And one more thing," Tina added as I stood poised to skate out for my performance.

"What?" I asked.

"Skate with your heart," she said.

There was no time to reply. I had to push off into

the rink to begin my routine. In the center of the rink, I struck my starting pose, with just a moment for one deep breath before the music began.

Once again, my mind shut down and my body took over as I glided into the opening moves of my long program. It was almost impossible to hear the music because the sound of my pounding heart was throbbing in my ears. My pulse and the slash of skate blades surrounded me as I went through my program.

"Here's her opening jump, a double axel combination," Turner Banks announced, although I barely heard him.

I spun in the air and, when I touched down, I knew immediately that I was off-balance. I was going over. *No!* I told myself. I couldn't let that happen!

I caught my fall by slapping my hand on the ice and pushing back up.

"Ohh!! She touched down," I heard Michelle Kwan say with a groan.

"When the stakes are this high, this is where the nerves come into play," Turner Banks said sympathetically.

I wished I hadn't heard him say the word *nerves,* because it just made me aware of being nervous.

I had to find a way to regain the points I'd surely lost by touching down. As I moved into position for my next jump, I decided at the last second that I would double it. I'd never doubled a triple flip—few skaters could—but I was willing to try.

I jammed my toe pick into the ice as forcefully as I could manage and willed myself to climb higher and higher still. It seemed to be working . . . but then I came down again.

I tumbled over backward, slamming down hard on my butt and traveling nearly a yard before I could stop.

The crowd groaned.

That was it! As far as my performance went, this competition was over. I'd blown it—big-time!

As I got back up to my feet, I glanced over to see how Tina was taking this. She sat watching, her face expressionless, revealing nothing. But behind her was another face that was filled with concern— Mom's.

She'd come to see me skate!

All these months I'd been telling her how good I was and now that she'd finally come, she was seeing this terrible performance! I had to turn this around somehow, show her what I really could do!

She saw me notice her and our eyes locked. I could tell that she was forcing herself to stop looking so worried. For my sake she put on an encouraging smile and waved.

I smiled back at her and nodded.

Suddenly, everything was all right. Mom was behind me whether I won the gold or didn't place at all. Nothing would ever change that—so none of this was that important, not really.

All at once I was a kid skating on a pond again and loving every second of it. I felt light and free and ready for anything, just as I had back then on those cold, sunny winter days.

As my spirits soared, I picked up speed, sailing around the ice. This might very well turn out to be my one and only competitive skating event. The chance might never come again, so I decided to make the most of it.

I leapt up and spun into a triple salchow! There's no feeling like flying through the air, turning at top speed. When I defied gravity like this it was as if I also broke free of everything else that ever held me down: There were no dirty skating tricks or treacherous competitors; no scholarships to be won and no colleges to be admitted to; no nasty "popular" kids; no skates I couldn't afford—there was only freedom!

I landed . . .

. . . and sailed off on one foot.

"Triple salchow!" Turner Banks shouted enthusiastically into the PA system. "Perfect landing!"

My footwork sequence came next and my feet seemed to know exactly what to do. The crowd began clapping along with the music, lifting my spirits even higher. I was actually having fun!

My program was nearly over but I didn't want to get off the ice. I was enjoying myself too much.

By then, I knew I hadn't won. I probably hadn't even placed—so what did I have to lose? I might as well enjoy one last jump. I'd make it big, a jump I'd always remember!

Off I went, launching into a triple lutz. And I followed it with a triple loop!

The crowd went wild, cheering and applauding.

"That has to be the rally of the year!" Michelle Kwan commented, shouting over the PA in order to be heard over the cheering, screaming crowd.

Turner Banks agreed with her. "Nobody's come back this far from mid-program disaster since Midori Ito in the '92 Olympics!" he said.

The crowd was still on its feet, cheering as I bowed and waved to them. Flowers were thrown at my feet while I skated off, still waving. I saw Ann and Gen screaming and hugging each other.

I spotted Mom, who was crying and smiling and applauding all at once. I waved to her as I skated past. By the time I reached the boards, my face hurt from smiling.

Tina was there to meet me. She was applauding as hard as everyone else. I sat with her in the kiss-and-cry area, awaiting my first set of marks, the ones for technical merit. They were high, especially considering how disastrous the beginning of my program had been.

"These marks are nearly identical with those of Nikki Sellman, who is currently in first place," Turner Banks told the crowd and TV viewers.

The second set of marks, the ones for artistic merit, came up on the scoreboard. "Again, almost dead even with Nikki," Turner Banks said. "Did she do it?"

In a second, the placement rankings came in.

"No!" Turner Banks cried. "She'll have to settle for the silver!"

"But only by one tenth of a point," Michelle Kwan added.

I hugged Tina, ecstatic. I sure didn't feel as though winning the silver was *settling*. In six months I'd be competing in the Nationals!

"After six more months of practice with me, you'll be able to whip her butt easily," Tina promised, smiling.

I got up to go and met Mom, standing off to the side. "I'm sorry," she said. "I should have come down to the rink. How could I not see?"

Her eyes were still red from crying and, when we hugged, both of us cried. But they were happy tears. "You see me better than anybody," I told her, meaning it.

We finally stopped squeezing and Mom pulled back slightly, regarding me seriously. "You'll go to school in a few years?"

I nodded. There would be time to do it all.

Teddy came into the area. He looked so amazing in a suit and tie. He held two dozen roses, which he handed to me. The next thing I knew, we were kissing.

It was my very first kiss and it couldn't have been more perfect.

Tomorrow would bring more hard work, more early morning practices. But right then and there, in Teddy's arms, I felt like I was in a fairy tale and I had become a beautiful, magical Ice Princess.